Marriage is About
LOVE

Divorce is About
MONEY®

The Bu$iness of Divorce®

Marriage is About
LOVE

Divorce is About
MONEY®

A Guide to Navigate Divorce and Protect Yourself Financially

By **Gabrielle Clemens, JD, LLM, AEP, CDFA**

Attorney and Certified Divorce Financial Analyst®

PLUMAGE PRESS

Paperback ISBN: 979-8-218-12288-1

Ebook ISBN: 979-8-9875056-0-1

Published by:

Plumage Press
4410 Plumage Court
Bonita Springs, FL 34134

Cover design, interior design, and production
by Happenstance Type-O-Rama

For You

*The person who picked up this book
in search of answers, as life
asks you to face tough questions about
your family, fortress, and finances.*

CONTENTS

ACKNOWLEDGMENTS

Many thanks to the ride-or-die people in my life without whose support this book would not have happened: Alfred, Marshall, Max, Mary, Sherry Ladha, Vita Melignano, Christina Ablon, Christina Pavlina, Caren Stanley, Heidi Webb and Julie Field, founders of The Consilium Institute, Lisa Austin, and Donna MacDonald.

INTRODUCTION

"I feel like everyone is speaking a foreign language," a client once said to me, "and you are my interpreter."

She didn't know it, but my client in that moment spoke for just about every person who goes through divorce. People experience divorce in countless ways. Sometimes divorce is a sober decision made mutually by spouses who have grown apart. Sometimes divorce comes seemingly out of nowhere, an utter shock to your system and your life. Divorce can be amicable, or rife with conflict and discord. It can move relatively smoothly and quickly through the legal and financial process or may drag on for what feels like forever. The financial decisions of your divorce may be fairly straightforward, dizzyingly complex, or somewhere in between.

For nearly everyone who goes through it, divorce turns life as you knew it upside down. And, at your most emotionally vulnerable, divorce asks a great deal of you. It demands that you be focused, rational, and disciplined when your emotions are running high and your family is in crisis. It asks that you think about the future when your past and present feel all-consuming. It requires you to learn and apply a great deal of legal and financial information that, for most people, is new and unfamiliar, and can be more than a little intimidating.

I wrote this book for every single person who is contemplating or navigating the divorce process and feeling confused, overwhelmed, or uncertain, for everyone who's ever felt—as my client did—as though they've been plunged into an utterly foreign land, with no guide or translation book in hand.

Marriage might be about love, but divorce is about money. Most people embark on divorce unprepared and unsure about how to make their best financial decisions, right when their entire financial future is on the line. I wrote this book to demystify the financial legwork of divorce; to guide you step-by-step through the essential financial preparation, planning, and decision-making in each phase of the process; and to give you strategic insight to make choices *during* your divorce that will help you protect your financial future long after your divorce is over.

Clients aren't the only ones who aren't prepared to handle the financial complexity of divorce. Lawyers are highly trained and knowledgeable in their area of expertise: navigating the legal process, applying the law, negotiating and drafting agreements, and arguing cases in court. Most divorce lawyers are not financial planners, money managers, or tax experts. Their lack of in-depth knowledge of financial matters can be a hazard for any person going through a divorce, and especially problematic for high-net-worth families, whose marital estates often contain intricate financial estate planning strategies, trusts, and executive compensation plans.

As a tax/divorce/trust and estate attorney and a certified divorce financial analyst specializing in divorce, I work with people at the critical juncture where the legal process of divorce meets financial strategy and long-term financial analysis and planning. I wrote this book to provide you with the information and tools you need to move through the legal process of divorce with confidence, to help you advocate for yourself and work with your attorney as an informed, assured, and effective strategic partner.

There is no way to take the stress, struggle, and strain entirely out of the process of divorce. But knowledge, and an action plan, can empower and equip you to work through your divorce and embark on your independent, post-divorce life with confidence, prepared to make financial decisions that serve you well today and over the long term. I wrote this book to help you do exactly that.

A Note Before We Begin: *It Depends.*

"It depends" is something of a mantra for attorneys and other divorce professionals. That's because the divorce process is complex and nuanced, and no two divorces are the same. Every divorce has its own unique facts, circumstances, and details. Your divorce is not your sister's or your neighbor's or your best friend's.

In this book I share critical information to help you better understand the divorce process and address the financial decisions many people face during divorce. How *your* divorce process unfolds, and the financial decision-making and resolution involved, will ultimately depend on the specific circumstances of your case.

PART ONE

BEFORE THE DIVORCE

CHAPTER ONE

"I'm Getting a Divorce?!"

Your Very First Steps

I f you're here, reading these words, divorce has entered your life. You might be quietly contemplating your options in a marriage that no longer fulfills you. You may be reeling from having your spouse tell you they intend to leave. You might be deep in the middle of an active divorce proceeding, feeling confused, manipulated, outlawyered, undereducated, and bombarded by details and information you don't know how and have never had to process. Perhaps you've finalized your divorce settlement, and you're struggling with questions about what to do next, how to move forward securely into a future that, right now, feels financially and emotionally uncertain. Wherever you are in the process, since divorce has entered your life you've probably experienced a range of emotions, from sadness, grief, anger, and disbelief to guilt and relief. And you may be feeling a lot of resistance to the changes that are taking place in your life, around the people and things you believe in, care about, and hold closest to your heart.

Divorce is about nothing if not change. Change is difficult and confusing, often painfully so. I describe divorce as the perfect storm, one that descends on everything that matters most: your family, your fortress (your home), and your finances.

I'm going to tell you something that may sound difficult to hear right now, when you may feel like everything in your life is falling apart. *Your divorce is a new beginning.* From the very outset and through every step you take in the process, you are creating the vision and the building blocks that will form the foundation of your future life. A better life. A life built on your dreams and your desires, and on your terms. Be prepared to be you again, but better, wiser, and more confident.

To navigate your divorce successfully, it is critical that you recognize it as a process of building your future. The financial arrangements that you make in your divorce settlement will shape the rest of your financial life. Taking a future-focused approach to your divorce helps you work toward achieving a settlement that meets your long-term financial needs and supports the vision you have for your post-divorce life. Keeping your focus on the future motivates you to stay actively involved in the work of your divorce, because you want to maintain control and influence over the decisions that are being made about your future. Throughout the process, take the opportunity to start planning for your new financial reality, and how you'll make it work to support the life you want to lead, a life aligned with your values, your priorities, your needs, and your dreams. It will happen; you will get there.

Focus on the outcome, not the obstacle. When your eyes are on the future, it's easier to remain calm and focused, and not take the bait, when things get tough in dealing with your spouse. Not because your feelings aren't valid, but because staying focused moves you closer to your future life, faster. Focusing on the future helps you to keep your emotions out of the work of your divorce. And keeping your emotions out of the work of your divorce is crucial to navigating the process you're about to undergo.

Vita was flustered as we settled into my office to talk. "I'm not usually like this," she said. After twelve years of marriage, Vita and her spouse, Taylor, had separated. Both had felt detached in their marriage for some time, but Vita had been the one to say, *it's time.* Immediately, she found herself overwhelmed by the process that lay ahead. She had worked as a graphic designer before scaling down her career when she and Taylor had children. Vita took freelance design projects part-time while being the primary caregiver for their three kids, as her spouse built their career with a cybersecurity firm. Vita co-chaired her synagogue's interfaith outreach council and led a group of parents in building a summer arts program in her town. "I'm the one who makes the trains run on time," she said, "and now I feel paralyzed."

"Sounds like you're the CEO of your family and your community," I observed. Her eyes lit up briefly and she nodded.

"Vita," I said, "you're going to take those skills and use them to run your divorce the same way."

The Business of Your Marriage—and the Business of Your Divorce

Your marriage has been many things. This is the relationship in which you built a family and a life. At different times in its history, your marriage may have been fulfilling—full of love, companionship, and satisfaction. At times it may also have been frustrating, lonely, and a disappointment.

Whatever your marriage has been to you, it has also been a business deal.

When you married, you and your spouse entered a contract that bound you together, legally and financially. *You established a business, and at some point there was a division of labor.* As your family and your marital financial life evolved, so did the business of your marriage. Now, with divorce on the horizon, your family is changing. And the business at the center of your marriage must change as well. It's now time to create a new contract, one that transforms and divides that business into two separate entities.

★ *Gabrielle's Pro Tip* You will be asked to make many decisions and take many steps to get from *here* to *there* in your divorce. Your first step is to understand and accept that your divorce is a business transaction, and that the fastest and most successful route through the process is to treat the work of your divorce like a business. Every constructive choice you make from this moment on will flow from this fundamental understanding.

The business deal at the center of your divorce is, in fundamental ways, like any other business deal—it has both legal and financial components, ramifications, and opportunities. But this business deal is also unlike any other because it carries with it a profound emotional weight. To achieve the best possible outcome, the journey you undertake through your divorce must address both the business and the emotions at stake.

The legal process plays out within the construct of the divorce laws of your state. These laws (and corresponding case law) provide a system with formulas and guidelines for dividing a marital estate (the property in a marriage), calculating child support and spousal support, and establishing parenting arrangements that serve the best interests of minor, unemancipated children.

You and your spouse will use one of several legal methods (sometimes more than one) to negotiate with your attorneys an agreement that resolves the financial and parenting matters of your case. If you cannot reach a settlement through negotiation, your case will go to court, where your lawyer will argue your side of the case, your spouse's lawyer will argue theirs, and a judge will ultimately decide how to resolve the disputed issues in your case. (In Chapter 4, I discuss the different legal methods you can use to resolve your divorce.)

The new business deal you're creating in your divorce raises financial issues and considerations that the legal divorce process is not designed to address. For example, you can negotiate a financial settlement that gives you sole ownership of your marital home. But the court won't consider whether you can truly afford to carry the costs of the home over the long term, or the capital gains taxes you'll be solely responsible for when you decide you need to sell. That is not the court's role in the divorce process.

A comprehensive divorce strategy recognizes the short- and long-term financial issues that exist in your case and addresses those issues during the divorce process to ensure your financial future is as secure as possible. A holistic divorce strategy asks: *Does the financial settlement proposal meet the requirements of your post-divorce life? Will you have the income you need? Have you agreed to divide your investments in a way that protects their value and minimizes your short- and long-term tax burden? Have you addressed marital debt with your spouse so you are not liable should your ex fail to pay their share?*

The legal process gets you a new business deal. But if you're not cognizant of the financial issues that underlie your legal case, you won't know whether the deal works for you until after it's signed, sealed, and delivered.

The emotional experience of divorce exists alongside the legal and financial process. Every person travels a different emotional road on their journey to and through divorce. Divorce is a transformative, often traumatic experience, one that leaves almost no person unchanged. It will test you emotionally, physically, mentally, and spiritually.

To participate effectively in the business deal of your divorce, you need to be able to keep your emotions in check, and out of the legal and financial work and decision-making process. I'm not suggesting that your emotions don't have a place. Quite the opposite. You need to be able to express and process your emotions as you move through every stage of your divorce. There must exist a safe, supportive, nonjudgmental space for you to be angry and sad, to grieve and regret, to rejoice and exhale, and to start the process of healing and moving forward into your future. When you don't address the emotions of your divorce, they inevitably spill over into the legal and financial process. Bringing your emotions into the legal and financial business of your divorce is costly and counterproductive and can negatively affect the outcome of your case. Emotions running through the business of divorce cloud your judgment and decision-making. They can make you unwilling to compromise when it is to your advantage, and too willing to concede when it hurts your position. Your emotions can drive you to seek revenge rather than stay focused on achieving the best possible financial settlement to launch your future life. And every impulsive, anger-fueled phone call to your lawyer costs money.

★ *Gabrielle's Pro Tip* You may want deeply to punish your spouse, but the legal process of divorce is not set up to deliver retribution. Focusing on revenge in your divorce will make the process slower and more expensive and will extract its own emotional toll on you and your family.

Think of the path to divorce as a railway track with three trains running at once: one legal, one financial, one emotional. When embarking on a divorce, you need a comprehensive strategy to get all three trains to their destination safely as quickly as possible, without any sloppy, destructive, expensive, time-consuming and unproductive wrecks that derail the process and cause harm to everyone involved, especially your children.

You are in charge of this deal.

I know this may feel daunting to hear, but you are the most important strategic partner in your divorce. Your actions and your decisions throughout the process will do more than any other single factor to determine the outcome of your divorce: how well your final agreement meets the mental, emotional, physical, and financial needs of your family over the long term; how quickly you arrive at that settlement; and how mentally, emotionally, physically, and financially prepared you are to enter the next chapter of your life when your divorce is final. The emotions and the magnitude of divorce can be paralyzing. I've seen many clients treat their divorce as if it were happening around them, as if they were bystanders to one of the most significant events in their lives. I've also seen many clients break through that wall, step into the process, get engaged, and take charge. You can do this. But you can't do it alone.

Your divorce team will be composed of professionals who can help you navigate the legal, financial, and emotional journeys of your divorce. First, let's look at your role, as the leader of your team. In your divorce, it is your job to:

TAKE CARE OF YOURSELF, MENTALLY, EMOTIONALLY, AND PHYSICALLY. You can't do the work of your divorce if you're consumed by the roller coaster of your emotions, exhausted, feeling negative, and running on empty. Commit to taking care of yourself throughout this process. Rest as much as you can. Fill your cup with things that bring you joy. If you have a spiritual or religious practice, lean into it for comfort and solace. Take breaks. Divorce is a marathon, not a sprint, and you need your energy and focus to sustain you for the duration. Divorce is a full-time job, and it can overtake your life unless you are deliberate about giving yourself time and space, every day, to live your life without your divorce taking up every bit of room in your schedule and in your mind. Practice gratitude every day. There is always something to feel grateful for.

LEARN HOW THE DIVORCE PROCESS WORKS AND EDUCATE YOURSELF ABOUT DIVORCE LAWS IN YOUR STATE. If you're like most people, you came into divorce with very little understanding of how the process works. What you know of divorce you probably learned from seeing your friends or family go through it. Before divorce entered your life, you had no need for this understanding. Your needs have changed. Throughout this book, you'll learn about the legal concepts, procedures, and methods that your divorce will rely on to arrive at a financial settlement. Every state has its own set of divorce laws that govern the division of finances, and case law that has tested the tenets of these laws. Your lawyer will advise you about how divorce law works where you live, but there is no substitute for educating yourself about how the legal process of divorce works in your state. When you understand the laws and guidelines that apply to your case, you empower yourself to be an active participant in your divorce, not a bystander.

DEVELOP A COMPREHENSIVE UNDERSTANDING OF YOUR FINANCES. Getting a divorce forces you to take a deep dive into your financial life. Once you or your spouse files a petition for divorce, you'll be required to provide detailed financial documentation. And you'll need to make countless financial decisions throughout the process: in your settlement negotiations, as you transition to two households and manage your finances with your spouse while your divorce is underway, and as you budget and plan for your post-divorce life. Your ability to make sound decisions relies on your understanding of your own financial realities.

KEEP THINGS CIVIL AND WORK CONSTRUCTIVELY WITH YOUR SPOUSE AS MUCH AS POSSIBLE. This can be a difficult road to travel, especially if there's a lot of anger in your divorce. But it is in your best interest to work cooperatively with your spouse as much, and as often, as possible. The more you and your spouse can agree on, the faster the process will move, and the less expensive it will be. Staying civil reduces the emotional toll on you and your children and leaves you with a better relationship for coparenting once the divorce is over.

Reality Check

The person you married is not the person you are divorcing. And yet you do know them best—you know what triggers them, what drives them, how they think. You understand what motivates them, and what makes them dig in their heels. That knowledge is a powerful tool that only *you* have in your toolbox, one that you can use to your advantage to simplify the process and promote cooperation throughout it.

GET ORGANIZED AND STAY SECURE. Staying on top of your divorce paperwork, deadlines, and schedules for meetings and hearings is a big part of this job. Set up a calendar to track your divorce commitments, and keep it up to date. Take notes on phone calls and meetings with your team, and transfer key information to your calendar immediately. It's important to make sure your divorce documents and communications are kept private and secure. Create a Dropbox folder to store your financial documents and other correspondence, reports, valuations, inventory of collectibles, and other information related to your divorce. Establish a new email that you'll use for all divorce communications, with an original, secure password. Use a messaging service with encryption, such as WhatsApp.

★ *Gabrielle's Pro Tip* Sign up for Informed Delivery with the US Postal Service (*www.usps.com*). This free service provides a digital preview of your incoming, letter-size mail (the address side of the piece) before it leaves the post office. It's a useful tool in helping you stay on top of your correspondence, including financial statements and other important documents related to your divorce.

BE YOUR OWN BEST ADVOCATE. Your lawyer and financial advisor have a fiduciary responsibility to advocate for you, represent you, and advise you to the best of their ability. Ultimately, your divorce is your responsibility. You may not have asked for it or wanted it, but it is yours nevertheless. Ask questions when you don't understand. Speak up when something doesn't feel right to you. Expect responsiveness from the professionals on your team. Listen carefully. Take notes.

Putting Together Your Team

Every person going through divorce needs professional counsel, guidance, and support for the legal and financial decision-making it demands. It's equally important to have professional support for the emotional turmoil your divorce unleashes.

YOUR EMOTIONAL SUPPORT TEAM

Throughout its stages and phases, divorce unleashes a spectrum of emotions: shock and confusion, anger and rage, sadness and guilt. Even the most amicable divorces can be emotionally grueling. If divorce was not your decision—and even if it was—you may feel profound resistance, the deep pull of denial, a powerful desire to go back to "before" and keep things as they are. The emotions of divorce can be overwhelming. Difficult as they are, it's important to know that all these emotions are a natural response to the intense, painful changes happening in your life.

You need, and deserve, compassionate, professional support to protect your mental and emotional health. It's also one of the most important strategic actions you'll take. Emotions flooding through the business of your divorce can negatively affect the trajectory of your case and your settlement. They will drain your energy and distract your focus, color your judgment, and compromise your decision-making. No matter how amicable or contentious your divorce is, getting emotional support now will translate into a process that's faster, less expensive, and less painful—a focused, strategic process that delivers you the best possible settlement.

Margo's story flew out of her in a single, anxious breath. On New Year's Eve, Chris announced he wanted a divorce. He'd already packed a bag and he left that night. Margo was completely blindsided. She knew her marriage wasn't perfect—whose was?—but she felt they were committed to each other. They both made a good living in their respective careers, but they had a lot of debt. And their two children were young, one still in preschool. They hadn't even started saving for college, and now their income would need to support two households. Still reeling from the shock, Margo was rushing to get prepared for what was to come. I was the first financial advisor she'd spoken with, and she was searching frantically for a lawyer. "What do I do next? What am I supposed to be doing right now?" she asked, holding back tears.

"The first thing I want you to do is take a deep breath," I said. "And your next step is to get a therapist."

Margo's eyes widened. "No, I mean, what am I supposed to do about all this?" she asked, gesturing with her hands as if to say, *this whole mess.*

I poured her a glass of water and handed it to her. "I understand, and I will give you the names of some excellent attorneys. But before you do anything, find a therapist."

A Therapist

With a therapist, you can learn healthy coping skills to work through the emotions of your divorce so that they don't overtake your life or your ability to focus on the legal and financial work of your divorce. You and your therapist will work together to help you come to terms with the end of your marriage and your new beginnings. Your therapist can help you navigate your ongoing communication with your spouse concerning your feelings about the divorce itself and about your children, household finances, and other family matters. As you work through your divorce with your legal and financial team, your therapist serves as a confidential sounding board and can help you stay focused on being a strong, grounded, determined advocate for yourself in the process. Your therapist can guide you as you shift toward your post-divorce life, and work with you to shape a vision of what you want your future to look like and the steps you'll need to take to make it a reality.

You can choose to seek out a therapist who specializes in divorce. Most important is to find a psychological counselor whom you trust, and who makes you feel comfortable, at ease, and supported unconditionally.

> ✔ **DO** make a therapist one of the primary professionals you add to your team. Regardless of where you are in the process of your divorce, if you don't have a therapist, get one.

A Support Group

Divorce can feel incredibly lonely and isolating. Your friends and family will show up as a source of support for you, for a while. They also may show up with complicated reactions to your divorce, and unsolicited advice that can confuse and misinform you about legal and financial issues. Even the most supportive family and friends tend to rally at first but eventually fall away as the divorce lags on and they start to suffer from divorce fatigue. Some friends will stop including you in social functions where spouses are attending. Other friends may see you and your divorce as a threat to their happy home and keep you and your problems at bay. You need support from people who understand what you're going through and will be right by your side for the duration. Divorce support groups provide a safe, compassionate place to share your anger and frustration, your fears and your grief. These empowering communities do amazing work to sustain people through the often-grueling process of divorce.

Many divorce support groups bring in professionals to educate their members on the legal and financial aspects of divorce. The more opportunities you take to educate yourself about the process, the more competent, confident, and successful you'll be as a participant.

A Divorce Coach

Divorce coaches have become increasingly popular in recent years. A divorce coach serves as your ally and supporter as you navigate your divorce process. They provide emotional support, help you prioritize your emotional health, and work with you to make sure you get the resources and professional help you need to manage your emotional journey through divorce. A divorce coach will encourage and guide you as you learn to advocate for yourself, help you clarify and address your questions and concerns, and communicate effectively with your legal and financial team and with your spouse.

There are training and certification programs, but no standard certification exists for divorce coaches. And divorce coaches have widely divergent professional experience and training. Some are trained mental health professionals. Some have training in mediation or collaboration. A well-trained, experienced divorce coach can serve as a bridge between the emotional and business spheres of your divorce—the person on your team who is familiar with all the components of your divorce journey, and supports you as you work through the emotional, legal, and financial process. If you think a divorce coach would be helpful to you, ask your therapist and your support group for assistance in finding one who meets your needs.

YOUR LEGAL AND FINANCIAL TEAM

You need professional guidance and counsel to navigate both the legal process and the financial issues of your divorce. When your divorce is final and a court-approved agreement is in place, you will walk away with an agreement you must live with for the foreseeable future. Under certain circumstances, such as hidden assets, agreements can be modified. However, once a judge has approved a division of your marital property, unless you can prove fraud there is typically no going back. To obtain your best possible settlement, you need professional help to develop a strategy that considers both the legal and financial circumstances of your case.

An Attorney

Your attorney is your legal advocate, your legal advisor, and your professional guide through the legal process and procedures of your divorce.

They are ethically bound to be your zealous counsel, to represent you throughout your case, and to advise you of your legal options at every step. With input from you and within the scope of the law, your lawyer will develop a strategy for your case and advise you on the method of case resolution that best serves you. They will negotiate on your behalf to reach a financial settlement, propose parenting time, and make arrangements for your minor children. Your lawyer can take legal action to protect you financially and otherwise during your divorce, including obtaining court orders to prevent your spouse from withholding money, to acquire financial documents your spouse is unwilling to provide, and to protect you and your children if your safety and security are at risk.

Most divorce lawyers are not financial experts. They will negotiate the division of your marital finances, with your input, or advise you as you and your spouse work toward an agreement in mediation. But typically, it is not their role to offer strategic, sustainable financial advice.

A Divorce Financial Advisor

A financial advisor who has expertise and training in divorce serves as the financial expert on your case. A financial advisor knowledgeable in divorce can work with you and your attorney to develop a sustainable financial strategy and offer guidance on how best to structure a settlement that considers your current financial realities and your future financial goals. Your financial advisor will evaluate your changing family's insurance needs, help you determine whether it makes financial sense to remain in your marital home, troubleshoot the tax implications of your divorce, and develop a strategy for your investments. They will help you compile the detailed financial information that will form the basis of your negotiations and review settlement proposals to determine if what's being offered meets your post-divorce financial needs.

I am a tax/divorce/trust and estate lawyer, in addition to a certified divorce financial analyst. But most financial advisors are not lawyers. They can't assist in drafting legal documents, make court appearances, or interpret case law. Your lawyer is your resource for legal advice. Your financial advisor is your resource for financial advice.

Who Comes Aboard *When?*

Your divorce may have been sprung on you suddenly, without warning. You may have discovered your spouse has moved through the earliest stages of the process while you were unaware. This leads to *divorce shock*, and it can be deeply painful and emotionally shattering. If your spouse has told you, out of the blue, they intend to seek a divorce, if they've hired an attorney or you've been served with divorce papers, take a deep breath, get a therapist, and begin the process of finding legal and financial representation. (I discuss the process of finding a lawyer in Chapter 4.)

Often, however, divorce comes more gradually onto your horizon. Issues in your marriage may have you contemplating divorce, or you may sense that your spouse is drifting away and out of your marriage. You and your spouse may discuss the possibility of divorce for some time before one or both of you decide to act.

When it is possible, there are advantages to doing some financial legwork before you hire an attorney or take other steps toward initiating divorce. Gathering your financial information and reviewing it with a financial advisor enables you to move into the legal process with an understanding of your current financial realities and your future financial goals. It gives you the chance to get your footing and begin the process with a set of clear financial goals. Beginning with the end in mind speeds the development of a legal strategy that protects your long-term financial needs.

Whatever your circumstances, I strongly urge you to find a therapist first, as you begin the process of building out your team. Establishing that central pillar of emotional support will ground you as you do the work of finding legal and financial help.

A Team Approach to Divorce Strategy

The relationship between your attorney and your financial advisor is critical to a comprehensive, successful divorce strategy. When this collaboration is working at its best, these two professionals understand the role each plays in the process. They respect each other's views and welcome each other's input. They collaborate without feeling intimidated or threatened. They also understand you, the circumstances of your case, and your future life goals beyond the divorce.

This kind of collaboration doesn't happen automatically. Some lawyers perceive the presence of financial advisors on "their" case as threatening and a loss of control. Lawyers may view financial advisors as interlopers who are involved in your case for their own gain. Not all financial advisors have expertise and training in divorce, and some may be more interested in selling you their insurance or long-term financial management products than in working with you and your lawyer to design and achieve the financial settlement that best meets your needs. In the next section, I walk you through the process of finding a divorce financial advisor.

This is your case, and nobody else's. As a client you have a responsibility to build a team that can work together effectively to advocate for you and represent your interests. Here are some steps you can take to ensure that you're building a collaborative team right from the start:

Ask for referrals from existing team members. Collaborative attorneys and financial advisors in your community know each other and have worked together. If you're already working with a lawyer, ask them to recommend a financial professional they've worked with successfully, have confidence in, and trust. If you're in a position to begin working with a divorce financial advisor before you hire an attorney, ask your financial advisor for recommendations for attorneys they view as a good fit for your case.

Hold an initial team meeting. Once everyone is on board, call your team together for a sit-down to discuss your case and how they will collaborate. This is an opportunity for you to see how your attorney and financial advisor communicate and do a gut-check with yourself to make sure you feel comfortable with the professionals you've hired to represent you. At the end of this meeting, you should feel confident that both your attorney and financial advisor understand you, your circumstances, and your goals.

How to Find a Divorce Financial Advisor

A qualified divorce financial advisor will guide you through financial decision-making, answer your financial questions, and educate you about the financial issues that are at play in your divorce. When seeking a financial advisor for your divorce, consider:

TRAINING AND CREDENTIALS. Seek to work with a Certified Divorce Financial Analyst (CDFA), or a Certified Financial Planner (CFP) with training and experience in divorce. Unlike CDFAs, not all CFPs are divorce-trained. If you're working with a CFP, be sure that they have specific training in divorce financial planning and that divorce financial planning is the primary focus of their practice. If you're working with a CFP rather than a CDFA, you'll also want to have a tax professional on your team right from the start. You can check CDFA and CFP credentials through the Institute for Divorce Financial Analysts (*www.institutedfa.com*), the Certified Financial Planner Board of Standards (*www.cfp.net*), and the Financial Industry Regulatory Authority (*www.brokercheck.com*).

Ask:

> *What specialized divorce training have you had beyond your certification?*

✔ **DO** check for complaints lodged against prospective financial advisors at *www.institutedfa.com*, *www.cfp.net*, and *www.brokercheck.com*.

EXPERIENCE. You need a financial advisor who is truly interested in helping you through the divorce process, not someone who is using divorce as a platform to sell you financial products. Seek out a financial advisor with experience in alternative methods of case resolution. If you have a divorce attorney, ask them to recommend a divorce financial advisor they've worked with successfully.

Ask:

How long have you been working with divorced people?

Do you specialize in working with certain types of clients?

Do you have experience in mediation? Collaborative law?

Have you testified as an expert witness in divorce cases? How recently?

Have you worked with my attorney before?

> ✖ **DON'T** work with any divorce financial advisor who seems impatient, easily frustrated, or less than entirely willing to take the time to listen and answer all your questions. Most divorcing people need financial education along with financial advice.

FEE STRUCTURE. Financial advisors charge using several different methods, and the type of fee structure they use can have a significant impact not only on the cost to you, but also on how your advisor engages with you and your case.

- *Hourly.* Every phone call, email, meeting, and conversation with other team members about your case is billed on an hourly basis. The rate varies depending on what's standard where you live and can range from $150 to $350 per hour. If you are consulting with a divorce financial advisor on a limited basis, then hourly billing may make sense. However, knowing you are being charged for every action they take on your case can have a chilling effect and make you reluctant to reach out when you need to.

- *Commission.* If your financial advisor is commission based, then they are likely operating a transactional business based on selling products, such as life insurance or annuities, or buying or selling your investments. It is human nature to question the advice of someone who earns money only when they sell you a product or conduct a financial transaction.

- *Assets under management.* This fee structure works when you trust your advisor's investment strategy. Assets under management requires disrupting the relationship that you have with your current financial institution and advisors, which may be fine if you are inclined to make a change from the advisor you and your spouse have been working with. During divorce, the tax implications of changing your investments requires particular attention—make sure that the advisor is knowledgeable about all aspects of investing, not just divorce financial planning.

- *Flat fee.* This is my preferred fee structure, the one I use and most often recommend. Paying your divorce financial advisor a flat fee makes you, and the resolution of your case, the priority. The advisor is paid one fee and works until the case is over. A flat fee relationship promotes open-ended, constant contact. It separates investments from divorce financial planning advice, enabling you to keep your investments intact until after your divorce, when you can think more clearly about who you want to manage your assets long-term. Fees can range from $2,500 to $15,000 and vary based on your location, the complexity of your case, and the time your case requires.

THEIR RELATIONSHIPS WITH ATTORNEYS. Divorce financial advisors and divorce attorneys work frequently together, developing ongoing professional relationships and preferences. You don't want to assemble a team only to find that your lawyer and financial advisor are like oil and water. Their successful collaboration is essential to your case, and to your peace of mind as you work through the process. Keep in mind, your attorney will charge for the time they spend talking with your financial advisor. And depending on how your financial advisor bills for their services, they may also charge you for conversations with your attorney. It is important for this collaboration to take place, but you'll want to be prepared for—and not surprised by—being billed for the time the professionals on your team collaborate. Consider putting some parameters around these conversations, including having them let you know in advance when they plan to discuss your case.

Ask:

> *Do you only work with certain attorneys?*
>
> *Are you able to work with my lawyer?*
>
> *Can you recommend a divorce lawyer you think would be a strong fit for my case?*

APPROACH. You're looking for a trusted advisor who will listen and be patient and responsive to your questions and concerns. You want someone who will take the time to educate you about cash flow, budgeting, investments, taxes, insurance, and other important financial considerations of your divorce. In your initial meeting, pay attention and ask yourself: Do I feel I'm being listened to?

Also ask:

> *How will you walk me through information I need to know about my finances and my case?*
>
> *How much will we be in contact throughout the process?*
>
> *When I call you with a question, how quickly will you respond?*
>
> *As issues arise in my case, how quickly can we schedule meetings?*

SCOPE OF SERVICES. You may decide you want to continue working with your divorce financial advisor on long-term financial planning, once your divorce is completed. This advisor will be thoroughly familiar with you, your financial goals, and your divorce settlement. If you've worked well together, that's a great place to start. To give yourself the option, take some time at the outset to understand their scope and approach to long-term financial planning.

Ask:

> *Do you provide financial planning services for after my divorce is finished?*
>
> *Can I see a sample of a financial plan? Can you walk me through how you create one?*

You're about to undertake the most important business deal of your life, at the most vulnerable time in your life. You have the power to set a course for your divorce, to set the tone for a process that minimizes the emotional pain to you and your family, to lead a team that works to deliver you the best possible outcome in a financial settlement. You can't control everything that happens in your divorce—including your spouse's choices and behavior. But you have more control than you think. Take a deep breath, seek out your emotional support team, and let's get to work.

CHAPTER TWO

The Numbers Tell a Story

Getting a Handle on Your Finances

Money is at the epicenter of your divorce. I don't need to tell you that, because if divorce has entered your life, you're thinking about money constantly, probably with a lot of anxiety and a whole lot of unanswered questions.

Divorce laws differ by state, but they all address the resolution of three major financial issues:

- How to divide your assets and liabilities

- Whether one of you will pay spousal support to the other—and if so, how much and for how long

- The calculation of child support from one spouse to another, if you have minor children

One of the most important undertakings in your divorce will be to complete a financial statement that lays out, in granular detail, all your financial information: your assets (what you own), your liabilities (what you owe), your income (what you earn), and your expenses (what you spend). *This financial statement is the most critical document in your case.*

It is a living and breathing document that should be kept current and updated often.

Financial statements from you and your spouse enable all the parties involved, your attorneys, your financial advisors, and the court to see a complete picture of your marital finances. And these statements form the basis for all financial negotiations toward a settlement. The time to begin gathering your financial records is now. Starting this process as early as possible will save you time, money, confusion, and frustration as your divorce moves ahead. Documenting your finances is a process that takes careful consideration and focus. And it is essential that the information you provide in your financial statement is accurate and complete, to ensure that you receive your fair share of all the marital assets you're entitled to, and that you are complying with the legal rules of your divorce. Accessing information about your shared finances is often easiest before your divorce gets underway; once you've separated, you may lose access to information about assets, debt, and income that your spouse manages or holds in their name or that is related to their employment. Often, spouses change account passwords, redirect mail, and close bank accounts to avoid transparency and exposure, all of which makes obtaining information difficult.

There's another important reason to start documenting your finances as soon as you can: to come to a full understanding about your financial circumstances. The role of managing finances often falls to one spouse as part of the many divisions of responsibility that take place in a marriage. You are likely one of two types of people:

> **YOU ARE HANDS-ON AND INVOLVED.** You pay bills and keep track of balances in checking, savings, and credit card accounts. You monitor your investments and retirement accounts. You have a good sense of what you own, what you earn, and what you owe. Facing divorce with this knowledge of your finances, you may be wondering, How will what we have support two households? What am I going to get? What will I have to pay? You're likely feeling a sense of dread, or defensive and guarded about keeping what's "yours." You're probably feeling scared and overwhelmed.

YOU ARE NOT ROUTINELY INVOLVED IN YOUR FAMILY'S FINANCIAL MANAGEMENT. You may have an incomplete understanding of what you own, what you earn, and what you owe as a married couple. Facing divorce without an understanding of your finances, you may be wondering, Where do I even start? What am I supposed to be thinking about right now? How do I know what these numbers mean to me? You may be feeling intimidated by the documentation process that lies ahead, and insecure about your ability to take command of your finances. You're probably feeling scared and overwhelmed.

🔥 *Red Flag* Every divorcing person is at risk for having unrealistic expectations about financial outcomes—and people who aren't dialed into their family's finances are at particularly high risk. Divorce is not a financial windfall, and almost no one who goes through it comes out on the other side without adjusting their lifestyle and their spending habits. The bottom line: you can't develop expectations for your divorce process and your post-divorce financial future until you fully understand the financial reality you've been living with in your marriage.

The work of pulling together your financial information will acquaint you deeply with your own financial realities, maybe for the first time. Even if you managed the money during your marriage, assembling a complete picture of your financial life is an eye-opening experience. You're probably going to learn a lot you didn't know, and that knowledge will be powerfully important to you going forward. You might be shocked at how much you spend on groceries, restaurants, entertainment, or travel. You may wonder if you have sufficient life or long-term care insurance to take care of yourself and your children down the road. You might discover your debts are more substantial than you realized. You may also discover that your spouse has credit cards or bank accounts that you weren't aware of. Nearly everyone who undertakes this step learns information that makes them uncomfortable and raises more questions. But every bit of this information and knowledge is a critical piece of the puzzle. Gaining an understanding of your finances *now* gives you the power to set financial priorities for your divorce settlement that are informed by your financial reality. It enables you to begin making projections about your spending, saving, and investing habits, so your financial life aligns with your values, priorities, and goals and the needs of your changing family. And it gives you and your financial advisor the data you need to create a plan to secure your financial future over the long term. Becoming acquainted with the story your finances tell isn't an easy process. But divorce will expose—and magnify—whatever financial issues and vulnerabilities exist for you. The question is not whether you discover them, but when. Far better to be proactive now—when you have the opportunity to work with your professional team to address the financial pressure points that your divorce reveals—than to be sorry later.

Who Decides How the Money Gets Split?

The answer to this question depends on how well you and your spouse are able to work together to compromise and reach an agreement. Once each of you and your teams have a complete accounting of your finances, then you, your spouse, and your respective attorneys may negotiate and agree on a plan to divide your assets and address your debt. Typically, your lawyers will draft settlement proposals and negotiate on your behalf, with direction and input from you and your financial advisor. Ultimately, a judge will review your final settlement agreement to ensure that it is equitable and treats both you and your spouse fairly, and that your children's best interests are being met in your case.

If you and your spouse are unable to reach an agreement on issues in your case, a judge will decide how those financial or parenting issues will be resolved.

In Chapter 4, you'll learn about the different legal "routes" to divorce and how each operates to facilitate discussion, negotiation, and compromise between spouses. Alternative forms of case resolution—mediation, conciliation, collaborative law—provide spouses forums to share financial information voluntarily, negotiate directly and informally, and work cooperatively to resolve their case. As you begin the process of working toward a final settlement, keep in mind: most divorces, in the end, settle without going to court. Negotiation and compromise are overwhelmingly likely to be the tools you will use to reconfigure your business deal and reshape your family. If you can negotiate and compromise willingly, civilly, and in good faith, you retain more control over the process and the final outcome.

Divorce Law Basics: The Laws and Concepts That Guide a Financial Settlement

As you learn about your finances through the process of gathering and organizing your financial information, you're likely to wonder—and worry—about how your case will end. *Who's going to get what? How much? How much will I have to pay? Will I have enough?* Living with these questions and uncertainties is one of the hardest things about going through a divorce. Before you begin to document your finances, it helps to understand some of the basic rules of the road in divorce law—that is, the legal concepts and guidelines that direct the process of dividing assets and debt and calculating child support and spousal support.

Divorce laws are state laws. Every state has its own set of laws and guidelines—and cases that apply and interpret those laws—that govern property division in divorce. Every state has its own formula and guidelines for calculating child support. And every state has guidelines and criteria to determine whether, how much, and for how long one spouse must pay, and the other receive, spousal support.

Divorce law is governed by state law. But divorce law is interpreted and executed in a local or county courthouse. Judges have jurisdiction of your case and must follow the laws of their state, but they have discretion in how they interpret and apply state law on a case-by-case basis. Let's look at the fundamental legal concepts and methods that states employ to regulate how financial matters are resolved in divorce, and how courts use discretion in applying those laws to individual cases.

> ✖ **DON'T** rely solely on your lawyer to educate you about the divorce laws in your state. Use the resources at the end of this book to educate yourself about how divorce law works where you live or where your case resides.

DIVIDING MARITAL PROPERTY AND MARITAL DEBTS

Once divorce enters your life, you start to hear the term *marital property* a lot. Marital property refers to the assets and earnings you and your spouse have accumulated during your marriage. In a divorce, marital property typically includes:

- Cash
- Investments
- Real estate
- Vehicles (automobiles, boats, motorcycles, RVs)
- Personal property, including valuables (jewelry, watches) and collections (art, wine, antique cars)
- Retirement funds
- Pensions (government and private)
- Employee profit-sharing plans
- Stock options
- Interest or ownership in a business

It doesn't matter whether one spouse holds the asset solely in their name or jointly. If you acquired an asset during the course of your marriage, especially with marital funds, it will be considered marital property. It is important to check your state's criteria for defining marital property. In all states, the definition of marital property is broad and inclusive. More often than not, the assets held by a couple will be considered marital property at the time of their divorce.

However, a narrower band of assets is considered separate, or non-marital, property. Separate property is not divided in a divorce settlement—the owner of the nonmarital asset retains that asset. Each state has a method and criteria for designating property as separate, but there are certain types of property that all states may (but don't always) regard as separate:

- Assets you or your spouse acquired before you were married

- Inheritances you or your spouse received before or during your marriage

- Gifts given to you individually, or to your spouse individually, before or during your marriage

★ *Gabrielle's Pro Tip* Prenuptial and postnuptial agreements may designate property as separate, depending on the asset, how it was acquired, and the intention of the parties who signed the agreement. If you have a prenuptial or postnuptial agreement in your marriage, make sure you have a copy and share it with your attorney and your financial advisor right away, so you can discuss how it affects your marital estate and your divorce.

There is a big, important caveat attached to the designation of separate property. *For an asset to be considered separate at the time of your divorce, it must have remained separate for the duration of your marriage.* Often, assets one spouse brought into a marriage are combined with marital assets. The legal term for the mixing of separate assets is *comingling.* Here are some examples of how assets get comingled:

Paul received an inheritance from his grandfather and deposited the funds in a joint account he shared with his husband, Rasheed.

When Tonya married Pat, she maintained a savings account she established before she married. The account remained in her name alone, but both Tonya and Pat contributed money to this account during their marriage.

Marcus owned a condo in Jackson Hole when he married Julie. During their marriage, Julie contributed financially to the condo expenses, sharing in the costs of repairs and maintenance.

Comingling makes the sorting of separate and marital property complicated, and it can become a contested issue in divorce. Every state has its own guidelines for distinguishing separate property, and judges will apply their views to your individual case in making decisions about what assets remain separate and nondivisible in your divorce.

> ✔ **DO** be prepared to document your separate assets if they become contested in your divorce. If you believe an asset is separate and your spouse does not agree, you will need to work with your attorney to provide financial records to the court to prove that your asset has remained separate property throughout your marriage.

Spouses share marital property, and they also share marital debt. As with marital property, timing is the key factor in determining marital debt. Debts generated by either you or your spouse during your marriage are typically considered marital debt, regardless of whether only one of your names is on the credit card, mortgage, student, or car loan. This will most certainly be true for debts either of you has incurred to pay for the lifestyle you've led as a couple and a family: debts generated from spending to run your household, care for and educate your children, and travel and vacation as a family.

Debts that existed before the marriage are generally considered separate, or nonmarital, debts, and the spouse who incurred the debt will be responsible for that debt after divorce. In some instances, debts generated by one spouse during a marriage may be considered separate—not marital—because of the nature and circumstances of the debt. A spouse who runs up substantial gambling debts or who, while having an affair, racks up credit card debt for hotels, restaurants, and gifts, may well find the court assigns this debt as their sole responsibility in a divorce, provided there is proof of the use of those funds. This type of spending is one form of what's known as *dissipation of marital assets* (or *marital dissipation*). There are other ways spouses dissipate marital assets, including:

- Transferring money from joint accounts

- Hiding assets

- Making large purchases with marital funds

I address marital dissipation further in Chapter 5. If you are concerned your spouse might be trying to conceal assets from you or remove money from shared accounts, take your concerns and any proof immediately to your lawyer.

When Do Marital Assets and Debts Stop Being Marital?

At some point, your assets and debts will be your own—and your spouse's, theirs. States have different rules for the crucially important date in divorce known as the *date of separation*. In some states, the date of separation is the day your final divorce agreement is filed with the court—meaning all new assets and debts you and your spouse generate throughout your divorce proceedings remain shared and must be divided. Other states define the date of separation as the day when:

- A divorce petition is filed

- You sign a formal separation agreement

- One spouse tells the other they intend to seek a divorce

- Spouses begin living separately in different homes

- Spouses begin living separately within a shared home

The date of separation has significant ramifications for your financial settlement, and it's important to know how your state defines this date as soon as you begin to consider divorce. I talk more in Chapter 5 about how to manage assets, debts, and spending during the period when you're working through a divorce but your assets and debts—old and new—remain shared.

States take two different approaches to dividing marital assets and debt. How your marital property is divided depends on whether your state is a *community property* state or an *equitable distribution* state.

In community property states, spouses are considered to own an equal share of all their marital assets and debts. Community property laws direct that marital assets and marital debts be divided in half. This doesn't mean that every individual asset and debt must be split in half. For example, one spouse may take full ownership of the home, with the other spouse receiving a larger share of the remaining assets. But in community property states, the overall division of both marital assets and marital debt is a fifty-fifty split. There are currently nine community property states: Arizona, California, Idaho, Louisiana, Nevada, New Mexico, Texas, Washington, and Wisconsin.

The remaining forty-one states use the legal principle of equity, or fairness, in directing how spouses' marital assets and debts will be divided when they divorce. Every equitable distribution state has its own set of factors that are applied to every individual divorce case to determine what is equitable and fair in dividing marital property and marital debt. Specific guidelines for equitable distribution differ from state to state, but many states will consider:

- Each spouse's age
- Each spouse's health and future medical costs
- Your marital standard of living
- Each spouse's current income and projected future income
- The value of your marital assets, and the value of assets each of you own separately
- The amount of your marital debts, and the amount of the debts you each hold separately
- Both monetary and nonmonetary contributions spouses have made to their household, and to each other's careers—such as supporting your spouse financially while they're in school, or taking care of children at home while your spouse works outside the home

Equitable distribution states use a different legal method to evaluate and determine property settlements in divorce, but the outcome is typically the same: a fifty-fifty split of marital assets and debts. In some cases, the needle moves one way or the other from a fifty-fifty division, but generally not by much.

Fault as a Factor

In some states, your reason for divorcing can have some influence over how property is divided. In every state, a person can file for a no-fault divorce. When you file for a no-fault divorce, you do not need to specify a reason for ending your marriage.

Most—though not all—states also give spouses the option to file a *fault divorce*. A fault divorce names your reason for divorcing, based on your spouse's behavior. Reasons for fault divorces include:

- Infidelity
- Abandonment
- Physical abuse
- Emotional abuse
- Mental cruelty
- Substance abuse

If you file for a fault divorce, you will need to prove the fault. In some states, courts will consider fault as a factor in dividing marital property and debt, and that may result in the spouse who is at fault receiving less than half of the shared assets.

★ *Gabrielle's Pro Tip* It is to your great advantage to go into your divorce process accepting that fairness is the goal, and that a roughly fifty-fifty split of your assets and debt is, except in extenuating circumstances, the generally expected outcome. This may not feel fair to you, but this is how the legal process of divorce works. You can drag the process out fighting for a slightly larger share of your assets and wind up spending far more in legal fees than you will gain from the additional share of the assets in question. When you can accept a fifty-fifty division as the goal, your divorce will move much more quickly, be far less expensive, subject you to far less emotional strain, and cause less damage to the relationships in your changing family.

DETERMINING CHILD SUPPORT AND SPOUSAL SUPPORT

If you and your spouse have minor children, it's likely that one of you will be expected to pay the other child support. The primary factors that determine child support are the parents' incomes, how much time the children spend with each parent, and the children's needs. In addition to income and parenting time, states consider certain expenses, including health care and childcare costs, and may also consider factors such as the children's standard of living during their parents' marriage, whether one or both spouses are responsible for children from other relationships, and whether they are paying or receiving spousal support or child support for children from previous marriages.

All states have formulas to calculate minimum child support. Every state's formula is different, and child support differs widely from state to state. States differ in the percentage or share of income they use to calculate child support amounts, and in the type of income they use for the calculation. Some states use parents' gross income (income before taxes and deductions) to calculate child support, while others use net income. Some states allow the child support payor to deduct their basic living expenses before calculating child support on the income that remains; other states don't. Child support is not taxable income for the spouse who receives it, and not tax deductible for the spouse who pays. States provide online calculators for estimating child support. You can find links to states' child support calculators at *www.alllaw.com*, or at your state's divorce law information and resources pages.

★ *Gabrielle's Pro Tip* Child support is intended to help cover the essential costs of raising children, and states have different guidelines for defining what is "essential." When negotiating your financial settlement, work with your spouse to create a plan for how you will share in all the expenses for your children. Your settlement agreement should specifically address the costs of extracurricular activities, summer programs, college and other education costs, health care costs not covered by insurance (e.g., therapy, orthodontia, vision care), and major events throughout your children's lives, such as bar mitzvahs and graduation parties.

Judges have discretion in establishing the amount of child support, and in some cases may choose to raise child support above the minimum guidelines. Circumstances that might lead a judge to elevate child support beyond the minimum include:

- The children's standard of living during their parents' marriage
- A substantial difference in the assets of the parents
- The children's mental, emotional, and physical special needs
- Child support agreements can be modified after a divorce is final, when either the spouse who pays or the spouse who receives support experiences a change in their circumstances, including changes to their income or parenting time.

✖ **DON'T** think you can shift to a lower-earning job to reduce your responsibility for child support. The court may look at what you have the ability to earn based on your recent work history and income. Your spouse can subpoena your employment records to learn why you recently changed jobs, and if you left voluntarily, it may reflect poorly on you and be construed as a strategy to pay less child support.

Spousal support is determined primarily by each spouse's income, the recipient's need for support, and the paying spouse's ability to pay. These are the major financial factors used to decide how much spousal support, if any, one spouse will pay to the other. Each state sets its own criteria for determining the amount and the duration of spousal support, but most states consider some or all of the following:

- Each spouse's age
- The length of the marriage
- Marital standard of living
- The health of each spouse
- Each spouse's ability to earn income, currently and in the future

- The difference between spouses' individual incomes
- Nonmonetary contributions spouses have made to their marriage and to their partners' careers

Spousal support can be paid in a lump sum as part of the property settlement, or paid in installments over an agreed-upon period. The trend for many decades has been away from the awarding of permanent spousal support. In many cases, spousal support is meant to function as a bridge for one spouse as they prepare to earn a living on their own. Spousal support is likeliest to last longer (or be a larger lump sum) when there's a reason the spouse receiving support cannot earn an income to support themselves, such as a spouse who has reached retirement, who is the custodial parent and staying at home to care for young children, or who has medical issues that impede their ability to work. At the federal level, spousal support is not tax-deductible for the paying spouse, and not taxed for the spouse who receives support. States differ in how they assess taxes on spousal support, so it's important to know the laws where you reside.

When There's a Business in Your Marriage

If you and your spouse, individually or jointly, own or have a financial interest in a business, that business may be an asset under consideration in your divorce. Business finances need to be documented, and the business may need to be valued. A business launched by one of you after your marriage will typically be considered marital property and divided according to the property laws of your state (equitable distribution or community property). A business started by one spouse before the marriage may be a combination of separate and marital property, with the value of the business at the time of the marriage considered separate, and gains in value made during the marriage considered marital. *Arrangements you and your spouse made for a business in prenuptial or postnuptial agreements may affect how the business is treated as an asset in your divorce.*

Be prepared to provide detailed financial records for your business, including at least three years of:

- Tax returns

- Balance sheets

- Profit and loss statements

- Accounts payable and accounts receivable

- Cash flow statements

Keep financial statements and records for your business separate from the personal financial information you're collecting for your divorce.

Add professional help to your team. In addition to seeking advice from a financial advisor, people who own or have an interest in a business will need to work with a business valuation expert and a CPA. The National Association of Certified Valuation Analysts (*www.nacva.com*) can help you find a professional to appraise the value of the business in your divorce.

Documenting Your Financial Information

The worksheets in this section guide you step-by-step through the process of collecting, organizing, and detailing your finances. When you complete this process, you'll be able to see—quickly and clearly—what you own, how much you owe, how much you earn, and how much you spend. This is time-consuming work, but it's essential. Doing the legwork up front to get your financial information in order enables you to:

- Clarify your *net worth* and the specific assets and debt to divide in your divorce.

- Develop an understanding of your *cash flow* and the income and expenses that will inform decisions about child and/or spousal support in your divorce.

- Be organized and prepared to complete and update a financial statement—on your own or with the help of a divorce financial advisor—once your divorce is underway.

- Be prepared to create a budget for your post-divorce life. (I'll walk you through the budget process in Chapter 5.)

A divorce financial advisor can help you with this process. Whether you're working with a financial advisor or not, undertaking a thorough documentation of your assets, debt, income, and expenses is of tremendous value to you as you move forward in your divorce.

Before You Begin: Get Organized and Stay Secure

Establish a Dropbox account (*www.dropbox.com*) where you'll store your financial records and all other documents related to your divorce. You can use it to easily share files and folders with your attorney and your financial advisor. As you work through the process of gathering your financial information, save all statements, bills, and other financial documents to your Dropbox folder. I recommend scanning copies of paper statements, bills, and financial documents and saving them directly to Dropbox. This is particularly important if you think you may lose access to information you need when you and your spouse separate or you inform them of your intention to divorce.

I recommend using Quicken (*www.quicken.com*) or another financial management program to organize your financial data, and for ongoing tracking and monitoring of your finances. You can input information about assets, debts, income, and expenses and build a balance sheet (aka *a net worth statement*) and track your earning and spending to see your cash flow. You can use the worksheets in this section as a guide for gathering the financial data you'll enter into Quicken. You can link your accounts to the program so balances are updated automatically and you always have a current snapshot of your finances. You can share information in Quicken directly with your financial advisor and your attorney.

You can also re-create these worksheets in Excel or another software program. **Be sure to save all your work directly and exclusively to your Dropbox folder (keep it off your computer desktop) so it remains private and accessible only to you.**

Many people rely on paperless (digital) statements for their financial accounts. And most people pay the bulk of their bills online. To access digital statements and expense accounts, you will need login credentials for those accounts.

Important Documents You Will Need During Your Divorce

In addition to statements for financial accounts, bills, documentation of income, and other documents identified in worksheets, collect the following documents:

- Three years of tax returns
- Wills
- Living wills
- Safe deposit box information (make a note of the box location, account holder(s), and contents)
- Powers of attorney
- Health care proxies
- Birth certificates
- Marriage certificate
- Prenuptial agreements
- Postnuptial agreements
- Previous divorce agreements
- Royalty agreements
- Patent agreements
- Copyright agreements
- Lawsuit records

🔥 *Red Flag*   You may find you can't access information you need for all the assets, debts, income, and expenses in your marriage. This is not uncommon, and often happens when accounts are in your spouse's name, you don't have login credentials to access account information, and you haven't been involved in managing your financial life. First, don't panic. Document as much as you can. Make notes for accounts you know or think exist. Your spouse will be required to share all their financial information with you and your attorney, and if they are unwilling to—or if they selectively withhold financial information—your attorney can take legal action to get access.

IDENTIFYING AND CATEGORIZING YOUR ASSETS

Assets are the property you own that has value. The money in your checking, savings, investment, and retirement accounts is an asset. So are employer pensions and other employment-based compensation, such as stock options and profit-sharing plans. The real estate you and your spouse own, the vehicles you own, and the personal property in your marriage are assets. In the following worksheets, assets are broken out by category, with instructions for the information you'll need to collect about each.

> ✔ **DO** list all the assets connected to your marriage. You may think some of your assets are separate, not marital. List all your assets, even if you think some or all of their value may belong to you or your spouse alone. Make a note in the far-right column to follow up with your financial advisor and your attorney.

ASSIGNING A VALUE TO YOUR ASSETS

For assets in your divorce to be divided, first each asset must be assigned a value. The value of assets fluctuates, of course. Your investments go up and down; the equity in and market value of your home changes. The divorce laws in your state lay out a process for establishing *valuation dates* for assets in divorce. *The value of assets on these dates is the value that will be divided between you and your spouse.* It's important to establish a current value for your assets and to stay up-to-date on it as your divorce proceeds. Quicken and other financial management tools can do this automatically. You can also get in the habit of taking a screenshot of balances in your investment accounts to stay current on their value. Physical property, including real estate and collections, may need to be appraised to determine a fair and accurate value. (So, too, may businesses you own or have an interest in.) As you do this preliminary work of documenting your assets, use a market value for your home, vehicles, and other physical property.

🔥 *Red Flag* Routinely monitoring the value of your financial accounts can alert you quickly if your spouse has removed funds to deny you access to them or attempt to hide them. Stay alert to significant or unusual transactions and sudden fluctuations in value.

ASSET WORKSHEETS

Collect your most recent statements for all your financial accounts. Save them to your Dropbox folder. Transfer the information to Quicken or another financial management program, or to your version of the worksheets below. List all accounts individually. If you have multiple accounts of the same type, list each one on a separate line. Add current balances to find a total value for each category.

Checking, Savings, and Money Market Accounts

ACCOUNT TYPE	FINANCIAL INSTITUTION	ACCOUNT NUMBER	NAME(S) ON ACCOUNT	CURRENT BALANCE	NOTES
Checking					
Savings					
Certificates of deposit (CD)					
Money market					
Total:					

Investment Accounts

ACCOUNT TYPE	FINANCIAL INSTITUTION	ACCOUNT NUMBER	NAME(S) ON ACCOUNT	CURRENT BALANCE	NOTES
Mutual funds					
Stocks/ETFs					
Bonds					
Other					
Total:					

Education Savings Accounts

Education savings accounts are tax-free (or tax-deferred) savings accounts that allow parents to save for education expenses. Funds can be used for education costs from kindergarten through college.

ACCOUNT TYPE	FINANCIAL INSTITUTION	ACCOUNT NUMBER	NAME(S) ON ACCOUNT	CURRENT BALANCE	NOTES
529					
Coverdell Education Savings					
Other					
Total:					

Retirement Accounts and Employee Benefits

Retirement accounts include funds you set aside directly in individual retirement accounts (IRAs), and retirement accounts established through employers, such as 401(k)s, 403(b)s, pensions, stock options, and profit-sharing plans. When gathering information on retirement assets, don't overlook military pensions. If you can, obtain copies of all employment contracts (if they exist), stock option plans, recent pay stubs, and W-2 forms for you and your spouse.

ACCOUNT TYPE	FINANCIAL INSTITUTION	ACCOUNT NUMBER	NAME(S) ON ACCOUNT	CURRENT BALANCE	NOTES
IRA					
Roth IRA					
SEP IRA					
401(k)					
403(b)					
TSA (Tax-sheltered annuity)					
ESOP (Employee stock ownership plan)					
Employee profit-sharing plan					
Employee pension					
Veteran pension					
Other					
Total:					

✖ **DON'T** panic if information about your spouse's employer-based retirement plans and other benefits are not accessible to you. Your spouse is legally obligated to share information about these funds with you in their financial statement. Collect as much information as you can. Make a note about funds and benefits you think exist as part of your spouse's compensation and follow up with your lawyer and financial advisor.

Insurance

If you or your spouse has life insurance, locate the policy information and add it to your Dropbox folder. Identify whether you have term life insurance or permanent life insurance (whole-life, universal). Permanent insurance may have cash value that is considered an asset in your divorce. If you or your spouse has term life insurance, it's important to know the remaining term, the amount of coverage, and the named beneficiary. Add life insurance policy details to the worksheet below.

TYPE	POLICY OWNER	BENEFICIARY	PREMIUM	COVERAGE AMOUNT	TERM	CASH VALUE	NOTES
Permanent life insurance					n/a		
Term life insurance						n/a	
Total (cash value):							

🔥 *Red Flag* Policy owners can borrow against the value of their permanent insurance, which reduces the value of the policy. Be sure to include loans against these permanent policies in the debts worksheet below. If you don't have access to your spouse's insurance policy, make a note to verify whether there is a debt against the policy when you and your team review your spouse's financial statement.

Gifts and Inheritances

Gifts and inheritances can be anything of value—including cash, investments, real estate, physical property, or collections—that you or your spouse have received from another person. Gifts and inheritances will typically remain separate property in your divorce if those assets have not been mixed with marital assets.

TYPE	RECIPIENT	GIVEN BY	DATE RECEIVED	FINANCIAL INSTITUTION	ACCOUNT NUMBER	BALANCE OR VALUE
Total value:						

★ *Gabrielle's Pro Tip* If you anticipate receiving an inheritance while your divorce is ongoing, inform your divorce attorney and consult with an estate planning attorney.

Real Estate

For many divorcing couples, their home is one of their most significant assets, financially and emotionally. Thinking about what to do with the house often generates a lot of anxiety. (I talk about how to think through this major decision in Chapter 5.) The financial legwork you're undertaking here, in documenting your finances, is going to provide you with critical information you need to make decisions about your family home and other properties in which you're financially—and emotionally—invested.

Collect property tax, property insurance, and mortgage statements for all your real estate holdings and save them to your Dropbox folder. (You'll use property tax and insurance information when you work on identifying your expenses.) Transfer information from documents to the worksheet below.

USE	NAME(S) ON DEED	ADDRESS	DATE OF PURCHASE	PURCHASE PRICE	APPRAISED OR MARKET VALUE	NOTES
Primary home						
Vacation home						
Rental or investment property						
Other						
Total value:						

Vehicles

Locate the titles for all your vehicles. On the worksheet, list each vehicle separately.

TYPE	NAME(S) ON TITLE	PURCHASE DATE	PURCHASE PRICE	APPRAISED OR MARKET VALUE	NOTES
Automobile					
Motorcycle					
Boat					
RV					
Other					
Total value:					

Personal Property

Your personal property assets may include home furnishings, collections of artwork, wine, antiques, coins, or jewelry.

DESCRIPTION	ACQUISITION DATE	PURCHASE PRICE	APPRAISED OR MARKET VALUE	NOTES
Total value:				

★ *Gabrielle's Pro Tip*   Think about the personal property that is important to you, regardless of its monetary value. Make a list of things you'd like to keep. Your spouse can do the same. If you and your spouse can agree on what you each will keep without involving your attorneys, you'll save time and money, and possibly build or retain some goodwill between you.

Asset Tally

To determine a cumulative total value for your assets, bring the total amounts from each of the asset categories to this worksheet.

ASSET CATEGORY	TOTAL VALUE	NOTES
Checking, savings, money market		
Investments		
Education savings		
Retirement/employee benefits		
Insurance		
Gifts/inheritances		
Real estate		
Vehicles		
Personal property		
Other		
Total assets:		

IDENTIFYING AND CATEGORIZING YOUR DEBTS

Your debts, or liabilities, are the obligations you and your spouse have for money you've borrowed throughout your marriage. Debts are either *secured*, meaning they have collateral that covers the amount borrowed, or *unsecured*, which is debt without collateral that is extended based on your credit history and your ability to repay the debt. Most divorcing couples have a spectrum of debt that is both secured (such as mortgages and home equity loans) and unsecured (credit card balances, student loans, and personal loans).

Debt is often a source of tremendous stress and confusion in divorce. The first step in reducing that confusion and anxiety is to know what your debts are. From there, you can make decisions about the best way to handle them. I talk more about how to protect yourself from your spouse's debt while your divorce is ongoing in Chapter 5, and strategies for dividing debt in a divorce financial settlement in Chapter 6.

DEBT WORKSHEETS

Collect your financial statements for credit cards, mortgages and home equity loans and lines of credit, student loans, and any other loans you or your spouse have taken during your marriage. List each debt individually: each credit card, vehicle loan, student loan, and so on. Add current balances to find a total debt amount for each category.

If you have debt you think is separate to you or your spouse, list it with a note to follow up with your lawyer and financial advisor.

Credit Cards

FINANCIAL INSTITUTION	NAME(S) ON ACCOUNT	ACCOUNT NUMBER	INTEREST RATE	CURRENT BALANCE
Total:				

Real Estate Loans and Lines of Credit

TYPE	FINANCIAL INSTITUTION	NAME(S) ON ACCOUNT	ACCOUNT NUMBER	INTEREST RATE	LOAN TERM	ORIGINAL LOAN AMOUNT	CURRENT LOAN BALANCE	NOTES
Home(s):								
Primary								
1st mortgage								
2nd mortgage								
Home equity								
Vacation								
1st mortgage								
2nd mortgage								
Home equity								
Investment property								
1st mortgage								
2nd mortgage								
Home equity								
Other								
Total:								

Vehicle Loans

TYPE	FINANCIAL INSTITUTION	NAME(S) ON ACCOUNT	ACCOUNT NUMBER	INTEREST RATE	LOAN TERM	ORIGINAL LOAN AMOUNT	CURRENT LOAN BALANCE	NOTES
Automobile								
Motorcycle								
Boat								
RV								
Airplane								
Other								
Total:								

Personal Loans

TYPE	FINANCIAL INSTITUTION	NAME(S) ON ACCOUNT	ACCOUNT NUMBER	INTEREST RATE	LOAN TERM	ORIGINAL LOAN AMOUNT	CURRENT LOAN BALANCE	NOTES
Student loan								
Personal loan								
Loan against retirement accounts								
Loan against whole-term life insurance policy								
Other								
Total:								

Debt Tally

To determine a cumulative total amount for your debts, bring the totals from each of the debt categories to this worksheet.

DEBT CATEGORY	TOTAL VALUE	NOTES
Credit cards		
Real estate loans and lines of credit		
Vehicle loans		
Personal loans		
Other		
Total debts:		

Your **net worth** is the total value of your assets, minus the total amount of your debts and liabilities.

Total assets:	
Total debt:	
Net worth:	

INCOME WORKSHEETS

For the most recent completed month, collect documentation of income paid to you and your spouse for the types of income listed below. *Gross income* is income before taxes and other deductions have been applied. Enter the full amount of wages and income payments for you and your spouse. We'll collect deductions in the next worksheet.

TYPE OF INCOME	MONTHLY INCOME (YOU)	MONTHLY INCOME (YOUR SPOUSE)	NOTES
Gross income from employment wages			
Gross income from self-employment			
Social Security			
Disability			
Worker's compensation			

TYPE OF INCOME	MONTHLY INCOME (YOU)	MONTHLY INCOME (YOUR SPOUSE)	NOTES
Retirement income:			
Retirement accounts (401(k), 403(b), IRAs)			
Pension			
Annuity			
Dividend income			
Interest income			
Trust income			
Royalties			
Rental property			
Child support from previous marriage			
Spousal support from previous marriage			
Other			
Total gross monthly income:			

List the deductions taken from your wages on the worksheet below. If you or your spouse is self-employed, consult your quarterly tax forms to find your tax and other deductions.

DEDUCTION	MONTHLY DEDUCTION (YOU)	MONTHLY DEDUCTION (YOUR SPOUSE)	NOTES
Taxes:			
Federal			
State			
Local			
FICA (Social Security and Medicare taxes)			
Self-employment taxes (income, FICA, Medicare)			
Pretax insurance premiums: medical, dental, vision, life, disability			
Health savings account contribution			
Retirement and employer benefit contributions: 401(k), pension, etc.			
Other			
Total monthly deductions:			

Net monthly income is your gross income minus your deductions.

	YOU	YOUR SPOUSE
Monthly gross income		
Monthly deductions		
Monthly net income:		
Total monthly net income (you + spouse):		

EXPENSE WORKSHEETS

Collect bills that exist for any of your expenses (tuition bills, gym/club memberships, home maintenance and repair bills, etc.) and save them to your Dropbox folder. Gather all your recent credit card and checking account statements and review them carefully to identify individual expenses throughout the month.

A quick tip: Use different-colored highlighters to flag expenses in the following categories—this will save time when you go to input the numbers to Quicken or a worksheet.

Home Expenses

These expenses cover the costs to own and live in your home. Use your most recent mortgage statements, bill statements, and checking account and credit card statements to find the charges that contribute to each category. Add together multiple expenses—for example, payments to different providers for routine maintenance costs—and include a single monthly expense for each category.

TYPE	NAME(S) ON ACCOUNT	MONTHLY EXPENSE	CURRENT BALANCE	NOTES
Mortgage or rent				
1st mortgage				
2nd mortgage				
Home equity loan				
Property tax				
Homeowner's insurance				
Renter's insurance				
Association fees				
Electric				
Heat (gas, oil, etc.)				
Water				
Sewer				
Internet				
Cable/satellite TV				

TYPE	NAME(S) ON ACCOUNT	MONTHLY EXPENSE	CURRENT BALANCE	NOTES
Telephone (landline)				
Housecleaning services				
Lawn/garden services				
Snowplow services				
Pool services				
Routine maintenance				
Major repair and maintenance				
Other				
Other				
Total home expenses:				

Living Expenses

Use credit card and checking account statements to identify monthly expenses for the goods and services you and your family rely on.

TYPE	MONTHLY EXPENSE	NOTES
Groceries		
Liquor		
Household supplies		
Dry cleaning/laundry services		
Clothing (yours and spouse)		
Personal care supplies		
Personal care services		
Pet care (food, supplies, medical care, insurance)		
Memberships and club dues		
Adult education		
Gifts		
Charitable donations		
Cash for miscellaneous		
Other		
Other		
Total living expenses:		

Child Expenses

Breaking out monthly expenses for your children is essential for when it comes time to calculate child support payments. And knowing what you spend monthly for child expenses will help you create a budget for your new household both during and after the divorce.

TYPE	MONTH	NOTES
Clothing		
Childcare at home		
Daycare		
Tuition		
Afterschool childcare		
Tutoring		
Program and activity fees		
School/program/activity supplies and equipment		
Transportation		
Cash for miscellaneous		
Other		
Other		
Total child expenses:		

Entertainment, Recreation, and Travel Expenses

TYPE	MONTH	NOTES
Dining out		
Catering/entertaining		
Events (movies, concerts, sporting events)		
Streaming services (video, music)		
Books, magazine/newspaper subscriptions		
Travel (transportation, lodging, dining, recreation)		
Hobbies		
Other		
Other		
Total entertainment expenses:		

Vehicle Expenses

List expenses individually for each vehicle you own.

TYPE	MONTH	NOTES
Loan		
Lease		
Fuel		
Maintenance and repair		
Parking/tolls		
Storage		
Other		
Other		
Total vehicle expenses:		

Insurance Premium Expenses

If, like most people, you purchase health insurance through your or your spouse's employer and have the monthly cost deducted from your gross income, **do not include that information again here.** (Make sure that information is included in your income deductions, in the earlier worksheet.) Here, list premiums for insurance you purchase directly with after-tax income.

TYPE	POLICYHOLDER	MONTHLY EXPENSE	NOTES
Medical			
Dental			
Vision			
Prescription			
Life			
Long-term care			
Disability			
Personal liability			
Total insurance premium expenses:			

Health Care Expenses Not Covered by Insurance

Using bills, credit card statements, and checking account statements, identify your monthly expenses for health care that aren't covered by insurance.

TYPE	YOU	YOUR SPOUSE	YOUR CHILDREN	NOTES
Medical				
Dental				
Vision				
Prescription				
Mental health				
Wellness services (massage, nutrition, etc.)				
Other				
Other				
Total monthly health care costs not covered by insurance:				

Expenses Tally

Transfer totals for each expense category to this worksheet to find your total monthly expenses.

EXPENSES	MONTHLY AMOUNT	NOTES
Home		
Living		
Children		
Entertainment, recreation, travel		
Vehicles		
Insurance		
Health care costs not covered by insurance:		
You		
Your spouse		
Your children		
Total monthly expenses:		

To see your monthly cash flow, subtract your total monthly expenses from your total monthly income. This will tell you whether your income is covering your expenses or you are spending more than you earn.

Total monthly net income:	
Total expenses:	
Cash flow:	

How to Get a Real Handle on Your Cash Flow

Breaking down income and expenses for one month gives you a valuable snapshot of your current cash flow—but it doesn't capture the full picture. To get a real handle on your cash flow, it's best to examine income and expenses over a longer period of time, looking backward and tracking forward. I recommend going back a full year to document previous income and expenses, while at the same time tracking current expenses for a period of six months. Your financial advisor can assist you in this. Doing this work on your own is an undertaking that requires commitment, attention, and time. It is also how you achieve a solid assessment of your cash flow and a deep understanding of your spending patterns.

Key Takeaways and Next Steps

- Start working on documenting your finances as soon as divorce becomes a possibility in your life.

- Take your time, be thorough and honest, and seek help from a financial advisor—but stay involved and engaged with the process.

- Get a grasp on your finances now because it is essential to being an active participant in shaping your divorce strategy and guiding the outcome of your settlement. Identify your net worth to see which assets and debts you'll divide in your settlement, and establish your cash flow to see how well your income supports your expenses.

- To understand how the financial issues in your case will be settled, you must understand how divorce law in your state treats marital property, separation dates, valuation dates, and the calculation of child and spousal support.

CHAPTER THREE

Your Future Starts Now

"What do you want?"

It's a question every divorcing person will hear, over and again. Divorce shifts the ground beneath your feet. Taking stock of your life as you embark on your divorce is a lot like looking at a jigsaw puzzle spread out across a table, a thousand small pieces waiting to be assembled. What will the puzzle look like when you put the pieces back together? One thing is certain: it won't look exactly like your life before divorce. Your family structure and your finances are undergoing significant change. You, as a person, will change and grow through this process.

Imagine being asked to assemble a jigsaw puzzle without seeing a picture of the finished product. You'd see only tiny glimpses of a whole picture, with no sense of how the pieces fit together. Imagine how much time you'd need, how much trial and error, how much frustration you'd experience to re-create even a corner of the puzzle, much less the entire portrait. You'd be working blind, going endlessly in circles, without that essential blueprint.

That is how too many people work their way through divorce, when they don't take the time early in the process to set a vision for their post-divorce future. Without a vision of your future, you are left to sort through countless details and make important financial decisions without an end goal in mind. And in a divorce, you don't have the luxury of trial and error. The terms you agree to in your financial settlement are ones that you will be living with in the next chapter of your life.

To make smart, strategic choices, you need to begin your divorce with a sense of what you want and what the outcome needs to look like. You need a vision of the life you're moving toward so that you can set goals as you work with your lawyer and financial advisor to develop a financial and legal strategy and prepare to negotiate a sustainable divorce settlement. Setting a vision of the life you want after your divorce enables you to budget and build a long-term financial plan to make that vision a reality.

The emotional turbulence of divorce can leave you feeling paralyzed, afraid, and adrift. That can be your experience even when divorce is a change you sought, a change you want. The upheaval and uncertainty surrounding your divorce may have you feeling as though now is the absolute wrong time to be envisioning your future. In fact, creating a vision for your future life beyond divorce puts you on the path out of uncertainty. It's a path that brings order and structure to your decision-making. It gives you direction and a framework as you work through negotiation and financial planning that result in a settlement that works for you, and a long-term financial game plan that will keep you financially secure.

You also need hope for a brighter future to get you through the tough times in your divorce process. Creating a future vision right now can do a lot to motivate and inspire you. It will lift your spirits and give you something to work toward. Divorce takes effort, energy, labor. It can feel grueling and exhausting at times. You need a vision of what comes next to keep you going. You need to be able to hold onto something that is yours alone, something that embodies the promise and possibility of your future life.

The routines, responsibilities, and compromises of marriage may mean it's been a long while since you thought about what *you* want. We all fall into patterns as adults. Our path is set (so we think), and we follow it, doing our best to live well, even when that means drifting away from our truest selves. You did your best to live well in a marriage that no longer works. Your divorce is an opportunity to reconnect with yourself—to rediscover what matters to you, what fuels your fire—and to recommit to pursuing those passions and priorities in the next chapter of your life. Divorce can make you a stronger, better version of yourself, and it offers you a fresh opportunity to define yourself and set your own path. But none of that will happen by accident. You need to be intentional about building your future life. And now is the time to start.

> ★ *Gabrielle's Pro Tip*   As you envision your life after divorce, give yourself permission to think big, be creative and playful, and have fun! If you could wave a magic wand, what would your life look like? How would you spend your time? Where would you live and what would "home" feel like? What would your community look like?

How Far Ahead Do I Look?

Everyone comes to the work of envisioning their future life differently. Take on what feels possible for you right now. You may feel eager and ready to think three years, five years, ten years down the road. *Go for it.* You may feel you can't imagine beyond a year, or six months, or a few weeks. *Do that.* Maybe you feel ready to take a truly big-picture approach, and think about all, or most, of the facets of your life: your family, your work, your retirement goals, your personal passions. *Embrace it!* Maybe you feel able to focus on one aspect of your life—relocating to a new home for a fresh start or returning to the workforce for more income and new professional opportunities. *Focus on that single piece of the puzzle and take on additional pieces as you feel able.*

> ✔ **DO** check in with yourself routinely to see how your capacity for vision work has shifted. You will be growing and changing continually throughout your divorce. You may surprise yourself, finding that what felt impossible a couple of months or even a few weeks ago now feels welcome, doable, and even exciting to contemplate.

> ✖ **DON'T** wait until life feels easy to take the time to create a vision of what's to come. There will always be something unexpected that crops up, a complication you hadn't anticipated, a frustration that throws you temporarily off your even keel, an obligation you weren't expecting, a task that needs attention immediately. That's true of life in general, and it's particularly true of divorce. Be kind to yourself, do as much as you can, and start today.

Pam was a client of mine whose divorce shock really made it difficult for her to imagine her future. Struggling to accept that her marriage was ending, she had little appetite or energy to think about what she wanted her life to look like after her divorce was finished. There was one place that had always brought her joy, where she felt most at peace and most herself: a sleepy, lakeside community where she'd spent summers as a child. Pam decided she wanted a house on the lake. Nothing fancy, she told me, just a place where she could retreat and unwind, on her own and with her adult children. "More than anywhere, that place feels like home," she told me. Right away, the lake house became a goal in the long-term financial planning we started during her divorce. It also became a totem of hope and renewal that she badly needed at the lowest point in her life. Identifying that one piece of the puzzle was an emotional turning point for Pam. She was able to focus on the legal and financial work of her divorce, and gradually was able to make other decisions about what she wanted from her life after her marriage.

When You Feel Too Overwhelmed to Envision *Anything*

Life can be overwhelming at times, and it takes energy to rise to the challenge in hard times. Divorce can bring a whole new level of emotional overload and leave you feeling depleted and without the strength and fortitude to see past the pain of today toward building a better future. Be sure to see your therapist regularly to take care of yourself emotionally, and be fully honest with them about how you're *really* doing so they can assist you with the support you need most. Therapy, rest, time spent with people who love and accept you, time spent doing things that bring you joy and a sense of purpose—all will help renew your capacity to focus on the future and the positive things in your life. Also:

- *Break down issues and tasks into small increments*, however small you need them to be to feel manageable. If thinking about a long-term parenting plan feels like too much right now, focus on the parenting schedule for the next week.

- *Focus on taking control of small pieces of your life to get through the day.* Get dressed. Take a walk. Call a friend. Keep up with your routines on the same basic schedule from one day to the next. Tackle the easiest item on your to-do list. Update your calendar through the end of the week, send one timely email, make one phone call, attend one support group meeting.

- *Track your progress and celebrate your successes.* Keep a daily record of what you've accomplished and take a moment, every day, to acknowledge the success of every item on that list, no matter how small it seems.

Some days will be better than others. But days will turn into weeks, and weeks into months, and with progress, you will be on your way to a fruitful, energized, confident, and independent life of your choosing.

Tools to Develop Your Future Life Vision

I'm going to give you a series of questions and prompts to get you thinking about the future, and your needs, wants, and dreams—and fears—for your life after divorce. This is not a quiz or a test. It's an opportunity for you to think about a future that truly reflects you—your passions, values, and priorities. It's a chance to discover what's really going on in your mind and your heart. It's a chance to have fun and get excited about what lies ahead, and how you can take action to make your vision a reality.

There are a few tools I often recommend to clients to help them tap into their emotions, think creatively, employ their senses, and explore the contents of their mind. It may be helpful to use one or all of these exercises as a starting point and return to them as you move through your divorce to clarify and refine your future vision, to see what's new and what's changing as you evolve and grow through this process.

> ✔ **DO** get a notebook or journal that you can use exclusively for the very personal work of envisioning your future.

START A CONVERSATION WITH YOUR FUTURE SELF

This is such a powerful, clarifying exercise, I almost always recommend it to clients as a first step in their vision work. Imagine yourself at ninety or one hundred years old. You've lived a fulfilling, rewarding life, accumulating all the wisdom of experience that a long life confers. From that wise perch of old age, you look back, with peace and profound perspective, on the life you've lived, the choices you've made, the roads taken and not taken. Ask yourself:

- *What would my future self want me to know right now?*
- *What words of advice, guidance, encouragement, and direction would my older self give my present self?*
- *What would my future self most want me to pay attention to and prioritize right now?*
- *What would my future self want me to embrace and pursue in the next chapter of my life?*
- *What would my future self want me to avoid?*
- *What is my future self most grateful for?*

Put your conversation on paper: write a letter from your future self to the you of today or keep a running conversation going in your vision journal. However you choose to engage in this conversation, it can serve as a potent source of comfort, perspective, inspiration, and gut-check wisdom as you work to build your future vision and navigate the complicated emotions and decisions of your divorce.

BUILD A VISION BOARD

Take a moment and close your eyes to recall a cherished memory, a time or place where you've felt happy, fulfilled, and most yourself. Whatever came up for you, you *saw* it in images: doing something you love, spending time with people you love, being in a place that makes you feel secure, energized, and alive. Our memories keep a powerful visual record of what matters most to us, combining images, color, and texture with emotion. A vision board is a way to depict your future in images that represent your goals, hopes, and dreams—to give yourself a tangible picture of the future you're working to create. In the same way that the memories of your past can point you to what you've held most dear, creating a vision board can help you discover what you most want and need from your future. Fill your vision board with photographs, pictures cut from magazines and books, swatches of color, and bits of text that speak to you and the life you're building. What belongs on your board? Whatever visual material inspires you, motivates you, and clarifies your sense of what you want from your future.

DO A BRAIN DUMP

If you're like most people going through a divorce, your mind is working in overdrive: keeping track of tasks and responsibilities, pondering countless questions, managing your ever-changing emotions, replaying the past, and ruminating about the future. That makes it hard to focus, find clarity and perspective, and establish the internal calm you need to run your divorce like a business deal and to be intentional about planning for your future.

A brain dump is a great way to get your swirling thoughts out of your mind and onto paper so you can make sense of them, and to decide where you most need and want to focus your attention—today, tomorrow, and down the road. This exercise is infinitely adaptable. You can use it to clarify your to-do list for this week. It can help you identify issues that are weighing on you and causing you stress, including emotional issues to discuss with your therapist, legal questions to raise with your lawyer, and financial concerns to address with your advisor. You can also use a brain dump to lay out your thoughts, feelings, hopes, fears, and questions about your future.

This exercise is as simple as it is powerful. You need a sheet of paper, a pen, and some quiet time to write. If you've never done an exercise like this before, I recommend you start by writing whatever thoughts, ideas, questions, or emotions come to your mind. Put your pen to paper and let it move. Don't overthink, and don't hold back. Offload the messy tangle of your mind to the paper. As you go, you are likely to feel the mental pressure and stress you're carrying start to ease. When your mind feels empty, put your pen down.

Once you get a feel for the exercise, you can do a brain dump for any topic, including a big picture of your future life, or any component of that future. Feeling confused about work and career in your future path? Going around in circles about how to handle the house in your divorce? Struggling to organize your thoughts about a parenting plan with your soon-to-be ex? Pull out the pen and paper and write it all down.

★ *Gabrielle's Pro Tip* To loosen up your mind, rather than making a brain dump as a list, try putting your topic at the center of a blank page and surrounding it with the thoughts, questions, and emotions that arise.

Questions to Ask Yourself When Creating Your Future Vision

These questions can help inspire and organize your thoughts and feelings about your future, and help you connect with the values and priorities that are most important to you.

WORK AND LIFE PURPOSE

What do you need in your life to feel fulfilled and content? What motivates you to get up, get dressed, and move forward in a positive way?

What is a basic requirement to be you?

What fundamentally separates you from others?

What do you want for yourself on the other side of this process?

What are you trading this marriage for: love, respect, self-esteem, independence, self-determination?

How can you foster and nurture these values and qualities in your new life?

What is the gift you could give to your future self to make this process worth the journey?

What did you want as a child that you can give yourself as an adult?

What makes you proud of yourself and your life: your home, your job, your children, your appearance?

Why do these things matter to you?

Where do you want to be professionally in one, five, or ten years?

What are your educational needs, goals, and dreams for the next one, five, or ten years?

> ✔ **DO** envision only as far out as you can see right now. Your vision, priorities, and goals will change and shift with time. You can return as often as you need or want to update your vision.

CHILDREN

What do your children need to feel loved, seen, heard, and secure? How does your current family life provide these things to your children?

What are ways you want to adapt your family life to help your children feel loved, seen, heard, and secure?

What traditions, activities, pursuits, and services are most meaningful to your children?

How can you maintain and/or adapt them as your family changes through divorce?

What new traditions, activities, pursuits, and plans do you want to create for your children as your family changes?

HEALTH AND AGING

How do you currently prioritize your physical and emotional health in your everyday life?

How do you prioritize your physical and emotional health in your daily life?

What does that look like in a vision of your ideal day?

What are your goals for staying healthy and aging?

Is your current home one where you can age in place?

Do you have long-term care insurance?

★ *NOTE* I talk about how to plan and budget for health insurance in Chapter 5.

HOME

What does your current home mean to you?

How do you feel when you arrive home?

What are the aspects of your current home that you love? What aspects do you dislike?

How can you re-create a version of those things in a new home?

What don't you love about your current home?

What new feelings, features, or aspects of home would you like to cultivate?

Can you downsize to create a new home experience where you and your children feel safe and secure and build new, positive memories?

Do you need to stay in your current town for the school system?

Is your current home appropriate for a single person?

Should you purge your current home and its memories by selling in your divorce, and rebuild your new life somewhere else?

What does your dream home look like? Use a vision board to bring your dream home into view.

★ *NOTE* I discuss how to evaluate whether you can afford to stay in your home in Chapter 5.

TRAVEL AND RECREATION

What is your dream vacation or travel experience? Envision where you would go, with whom, and what you would do there.

How long do you travel for? How often?

Do you like to mix with the locals or enjoy luxurious vacations at a high-end resort?

Do you want to experience culture, environment, or challenging trips?

Do you travel alone? Do you prefer active vacations or relaxing ones?

Hotel or hostel?

What is your typical trip budget?

Make a vision board for a trip that makes you happy, rejuvenated, and satisfied when you return home. What does that look like?

RETIREMENT

How do you envision your lifestyle in retirement?

Where would you like to live when you're retired?

What do you envision as being your primary activity in retirement?

Do you imagine yourself being active or relaxing?

What would an ideal day in retirement look like for you? Build a vision board of a day in your retired life. Get specific, use pictures that resonate with you, and don't be afraid to dream!

Do you have a plan for retirement?

★ *NOTE* I talk about options for dividing retirement funds in your divorce settlement in Chapter 6 and planning for retirement after your divorce in Chapter 9.

ESTATE PLANNING

Who are trusted, fiduciary individuals in your life?

Who do you trust to manage your money, make financial decisions, care for your children, and manage your assets if you were to become incapacitated or pass away?

Do you have a favorite charitable organization or entity that you would like to support in the future?

Do you have a trust?

Do you have life insurance?

What people or entities would you like to support when you die?

How can your money support your values when you pass away?

★ *NOTE*   In Chapter 6, I talk about life insurance as a component of your divorce settlement. In Chapter 9, I walk you through the basics of estate planning after a divorce.

Facing Your Fears as You Move Forward

Creating a vision for your future also involves taking a closer look at your fears. Divorce brings up a lot of fear, especially about money. By documenting your finances, you've taken a very important, very necessary deep dive into your financial circumstances. Having taken a close look at your finances, you may be asking yourself, "Am I going to be okay?" The financial fear and uncertainty wrapped up in divorce can be exhausting. Left unaddressed, fear and anxiety can cloud your ability to think clearly and make rational decisions. When you take time to examine your fears, they can be incredibly instructive.

Many of us have a fear-based relationship to money that long predates divorce. The change and uncertainty of divorce can intensify and complicate those financial fears. Taking time now to identify the fears you're carrying can motivate you to make necessary adjustments to your spending, focus your attention on budgeting and long-term financial planning, and help you set goals and priorities for your financial settlement. Here are some basic dos and don'ts for handling your financial fears:

DON'T AVOID THEM. Avoidance only amplifies fear. Don't put off your fears. Instead, be deliberate about identifying your fears and concerns as you envision your future life. What keeps you up at night? Put words to your fears and write them down. Be specific. The more clarity you can bring to your understanding of your fears, the better able you are to develop a plan to address them.

WALK THROUGH OUTCOMES. Ask yourself: What is the worst that could happen if my fear is realized? And what comes next? Playing out scenarios can put fears into perspective and help you to understand what actions you need to take to avoid worst-case (and even not-so-great) outcomes. Walking yourself through potential outcomes will motivate you to focus on finding solutions, and build your confidence in your ability to be an independent financial decision maker and problem solver.

DON'T GO IT ALONE. Your emotional support team exists to help you identify and process the fears that come up for you in your divorce. Work with your therapist to clarify your fears and understand their source. Your therapist can help you develop coping skills to manage your emotions, put your fears in perspective, and set realistic expectations for addressing your fears constructively. Your therapist can also work with you to identify the issues to raise with your lawyer and your financial advisor. And by processing your emotions with your therapist, you will be able to engage with your attorney and your financial advisor with a focused, centered, solutions-oriented business mindset. Your support group is a community to lean on for comfort and to remind you that no matter what your fears are, you are not alone in experiencing them. You'll learn practical problem-solving skills from people who've walked the path you're on and be inspired by others' success in overcoming the fears and hurdles that they faced in their divorces.

Your financial circumstances are unique to you, but there are fundamental financial anxieties that come up often in a divorce. You may recognize yourself in one or more of these common financial fears.

I WON'T HAVE ENOUGH INCOME TO LIVE ON

A careful assessment of both your current financial position and your future, post-divorce financial position is critical to understanding how your financial settlement agreement is going to impact your life. This is why it's so important to get a handle on your finances as quickly as possible. The sooner you're working with a hands-on understanding of your cash flow and your net worth, the better you're able to work proactively to negotiate a settlement that protects you financially, and start working to establish a long-term plan for your financial future.

Two households are more expensive than one. This is a basic reality of divorce that nobody avoids. It is likely that coming out of your divorce, your cash flow will change. Once you have completed your financial statement, you are in a position to plan and make decisions and adjustments to bring your expenses in line with your income. You can determine whether you can afford to stay in your marital home. If you're not currently working outside the home, you can start making plans for entering the workforce, part-time or full-time. You can start planning and setting goals for contributing to retirement, saving for college, buying a new car, and taking vacations. If your anticipated cash flow is negative (more money going out than coming in), you have two tools to rectify that problem: reduce your expenses and/or increase your income.

In Chapter 5, I walk you through the process of creating a budget, share strategies for reducing expenses, and troubleshoot the financial transition from one household to two.

★ *Gabrielle's Pro Tip*   If you are anticipating receiving spousal or child support, you can use your state's calculators to estimate the amounts you are likely to receive based on your income and your spouse's income. (Until your divorce agreement is final, there are no guarantees that the projected amount will be the final amount.) Since spousal and child support calculations are based on income, be aware that when income changes significantly, you or your spouse may file for a modification, which means that support can change. If you anticipate receiving child or spousal support and are planning a return to the workforce or an increase in your earned income after your divorce, discuss these plans with your lawyer and financial advisor, so you can understand and prepare for how your support may change over time.

MY LIFESTYLE IS GOING TO CHANGE

Yes, it will change. And it can change for the better. Once your divorce is final, you will have a new lifestyle to enjoy, without the stress and strain of an unhappy marriage. Ask yourself: *What is that worth to me? What do I value? Do I want experiences or things?*

The longer you ponder the past, the longer you put off your happiness and a bright, confident future for yourself and your family. Many of my clients tell me that as a result of their divorce, they get to be themselves again, but better. They have the freedom to pursue the things that they like, enjoy the food that they prefer, and live their life free from the constraints of a conflicted relationship. They get to make new rules, ones where they decide what works and what doesn't. What a great opportunity to create the future you dream of.

> ✖ **DON'T** lose sight of what you're gaining by moving on from your marriage. In your journal, make a list of what you are willing to exchange for peace of mind and the freedom to make your life what you want it to be. Refer to it as often as you need, to remind yourself of what you're working toward.

I WON'T BE ABLE TO STAY IN MY HOME

Do you want to stay in your home? Many of my clients prefer moving with their children to a new home to build new, happy memories together. I had a client who felt very strongly about remaining in her marital home, in the town where her children grew up, so her kids could come "home" on breaks from college, stay in their rooms, and see their friends. She spent a lot of money in real estate taxes and homeowners' insurance to live in an expensive community where she no longer needed to reside. Guess what? The kids rarely came home for more than a week or two. College semesters abroad, summer internships, time with their other parent, and their weekend social plans took the kids to exciting and sometimes faraway places. My client, meanwhile, was stuck at home, paying to live in the past rather than building her own future. She felt left behind. She struggled financially and grew resentful of her children for not appreciating her sacrifices. Eventually, she sold the house. She moved twenty-five years' worth of her family's belongings by herself. She moved to a new home in a community where she has friends and room for the kids when they visit. The move freed up money for her to travel and enjoy her life again.

Eventually, everyone moves. Your divorce may mean you will move sooner than you expected. Accept and embrace that change as an opportunity to make a new home truly your own. Envision your new space with your favorite colors, furniture, décor, and landscaping. Whatever four walls you live within, you make a home through the relationships, experiences, and atmosphere that fill the space. Envision a home where you are proud to entertain friends, enjoy the holidays, and be yourself. Surround yourself with the music, books, and art you prefer and photos of the things and people you love.

I WON'T BE ABLE TO PAY FOR MY KIDS' COLLEGE

Paying for college takes planning and, often, a multipronged approach. Start planning now and include your children in the conversation. Depending on how old they are, a 529 college savings account may make sense. If your children are within a year or two of graduating high school, it may be too late to reap the benefits of 529s and other education savings accounts. If you own a home, you may be able to take a home equity line of credit (HELOC) to pay for college; you will have to pay it back with interest or it will be repaid when you sell the house. File the Free Application for Federal Student Aid (FAFSA, at *www.studentaid.gov*) to apply for state and federal assistance via grants, parent loans (PLUS), and student loans. Some students take courses at an affordable community college, get good grades, and transfer those credits to a college of their choice, which can lower the total costs. You might structure your agreement with your spouse so that they pay for college and you will pay for other expenses such as travel costs, computers, and books. Depending on the divorce laws in your state, you may be able to include college funding in your agreement. Some parents require their children to help by taking out student loans.

If you are committed to paying for college and you don't have the funds, consider getting a job to cover the costs. Working has a wonderful way of providing structure to your day, broadening your horizons, helping you meet new people, and getting you out of your own head. Several of my clients have taken jobs at their local universities, where often employees' children can attend for free.

To clarify your thinking about how you want to approach funding your children's college education, ask yourself:

- *Did I pay for some or all of my own college?*
- *Did I work during college?*
- *Do I expect to pay for some or all of my child's college?*
- *Have I saved money for college expenses? Is this a priority I want to set in my divorce agreement?*
- *Do I expect my child to work during college?*
- *What would happen if I or my child had to take out a loan to pay for college?*

I WON'T BE ABLE TO RETIRE

Register for your Social Security benefits at *www.ssa.gov*. Check your benefits based on your work record, all the way back to your first job. If you were married to your spouse for ten years or longer, you are entitled to 50 percent of their Social Security benefit or 100 percent of yours—not both—once you and your ex-spouse reach the age of eligibility. To receive 50 percent of your ex-spouse's Social Security, you must be unmarried at the time you are eligible and have been divorced for at least two years. If you opt to take your own Social Security benefit, you may do so whether or not you are married as long as you've reached the age of eligibility. As you approach age sixty-two, call or visit the Social Security office in your area to review your benefits options. You will need your ex-spouse's Social Security number.

Work with a qualified divorce financial advisor throughout your divorce to create a financial plan that takes inventory of your retirement assets, projects their future value and tax consequences, and projects your income, expenses, and Social Security benefit to get an accurate picture of your long-term financial future.

In Chapter 9, I walk you through the fundamental steps of long-term financial planning after a divorce.

When Vita and Taylor started a family, Vita was the one to take a step back from her career. Vita's freelance graphic design work, which she loved, had allowed her to be flexible and work around the kids' schedules, but she'd always anticipated working more when the kids were older. Now, embarking on her divorce and contemplating her future, Vita felt new urgency in being able to work more, both for her personal fulfillment and for the income she knew she'd need.

Vita had jumped in quickly to organize her financial information; she found it helped her move past the initial paralysis that she'd felt when she first realized it was time for her and Taylor to move ahead with divorce. They were doing their best to keep things amicable between them. They were separated but still living together in their home. They'd even worked together over a few late nights in their kitchen, after their kids were asleep, to sort through their financial accounts and income statements. Vita felt good about what they'd accomplished and that they were communicating with each other reasonably well. But she was concerned about their cash flow when they transitioned to two homes. Vita spent nights tossing and turning, her mind going in circles over whether to stay in their home or sell it, and whether she could earn enough income to make things work while still taking on primary responsibility for their kids. Until a couple of years ago, she and Taylor had taken turns getting the kids to preschool, taking care of the house, and preparing meals. Then Taylor began to travel more for work, which left Vita increasingly responsible for taking care of the kids during the week. It was one of the issues that had contributed to their split, and now Vita found herself experiencing new levels of resentment over Taylor's continued reliance on her to meet their children's daily needs while Taylor pursued their professional ambitions.

Talking things through with her therapist, Vita understood that she needed to focus on creating a parenting plan that gave them both meaningful time—and responsibility—with their children. Both she and Taylor were meeting with family law attorneys, and Vita was hopeful they could work out their financial and parenting issues without going to court. And she realized it was time to start mapping out her income and expenses for when Taylor moved out. Should she go back to an office full-time? After taking time to think about the next chapter in her life, she discovered that what she really wanted was to build her freelance design business. But she wondered if that would provide her with enough money. When she came to my office, she was ready to talk through her options.

She had documentation of Taylor's income as well as her own, so we were able to run the numbers for child support based on her state's formula to get a projection. Vita anticipated she would be the primary parent, but she didn't know yet how much time the kids would spend with Taylor, and that would affect both her child support and her ability to grow her design business. Reducing her expenses would help close the income gap she anticipated, but it wasn't going to get her all the way there. She was open to selling the house—"We can live happily in a new place with a little less space; we don't need to stay here" —but she'd need to find a new home in a nearby town with a good school system so she and Taylor could easily share parenting time and responsibility. And she needed some dedicated space at home for her office. Based on the length of their marriage and the difference in their current incomes, Vita was eligible for spousal support, which could help her bridge the gap while she developed her client base and increased her income. She also had to consider how increasing her income by growing her business could affect Taylor's child support payments over time. Vita had a growing sense of what the big picture of her puzzle looked like, and the individual jigsaw pieces were beginning to come into focus. Her next steps—in consultation with her lawyer and with me, and in negotiations with Taylor—were to begin to figure out how best to fit them together.

Key Takeaways and Next Steps

Your vision for your future will shape your goals for your divorce settlement and your financial planning to prepare for the next chapter of your life. This vision work establishes the big picture of the puzzle that you'll be working to assemble.

- As you begin to envision your post-divorce future, take on as much as you feel able to imagine right now. As you move through your divorce, check in with yourself regularly to see how your capacity for developing a future vision has grown.

- Discuss your thoughts, ideas, dreams, and fears about the future with your therapist. They will help you organize your thoughts, process your emotions, and clarify your goals.

- Talk with your lawyer and financial advisor about your goals and priorities for your future so they can use that information in developing a legal and financial strategy to help you reach those goals.

CHAPTER FOUR

Identifying Your Best Route to Divorce— and the Right Lawyer to Get You There

"I feel like I am losing my mind," a client said to me recently, looking baffled and overwhelmed. He was early in his divorce, consulting with prospective attorneys and getting a lot of unsolicited advice from family and friends about whom to hire and which legal process to use. *Get a shark—you're going to need one in court! Stay out of court, whatever you do! You must mediate; keep the lawyers out of it! Whatever you do, don't use mediation—my cousin got totally robbed! Make your attorney negotiate! Don't let your attorney negotiate—do it yourself; you'll save so much!*

> ✖ **DON'T** assume that the process that worked (or didn't work) for your cousin's or your dad's or your coworker's divorce is the right (or wrong) option for you. Every case is different. Educate yourself about how each divorce process works, be honest and realistic about the circumstances of your case and your ability to work with your spouse, and choose the process and the attorney that feels right for you.

When it comes to the legal process, all divorces end at the same destination: with the legal termination of a marriage and a division of marital property (as well as child and/or spousal support and parenting arrangements when applicable). But there are several legal paths that you can use to settle your case. There is no one right or wrong method to settle divorce cases. Litigation, mediation, arbitration, collaborative law: Each employs a different process for bringing cases to a final agreement. Each relies on different tools to help keep cases on track, and uses divorce professionals (lawyers, judges, financial advisors, accountants, divorce coaches, and others) in different ways. The right method for your case is the one that gets you a fair financial settlement and resolves child-related issues as quickly as possible, while keeping costs as low as possible and minimizing the emotional stress and strain as much as possible. How do you know which path is right for you?

> ✔ **DO** keep in mind that your ability to work cooperatively with your spouse is the single most important factor in determining which case resolution method you'll be able to use. And no matter which route you take, your ability to remain civil, follow the rules, and focus on the business matters at the center of your divorce will have a major impact on the time the process takes and how much it costs you.

Your lawyer is your guide and advocate through the legal labyrinth of divorce, and selecting a lawyer with the skills, experience, and approach that best suits your case is critical. How do you go about finding a lawyer whom you trust and who meets the needs of your case?

In this chapter, I review your options for resolving your case, providing an overview of each process, a rundown of its benefits and drawbacks, and factors to consider. I also walk you through the most important considerations when choosing a lawyer for your divorce.

★ *Gabrielle's Pro Tip*   Before you meet with prospective attorneys, it can be helpful to understand the basics of case resolution methods and have a sense of which one you think suits your case. When you know which path you want to take in your divorce, you're in a better position to select an attorney whose experience and approach suits your needs and interests.

It's important to understand that sometimes a case requires more than one method to reach a full and final agreement. You may begin in a collaborative law process and, if it doesn't work to resolve your issues, move to litigation. You might use mediation to resolve the parenting and basic financial issues in your case and decide to litigate (or arbitrate) a specific financial point of dispute. As you consider what's best for your case, be aware that sometimes a route change is necessary to come to a final agreement. You have some flexibility and control to "mix and match" methods to suit the components of your case.

Using Litigation to Divorce

Litigation is the process of resolving your divorce case through the family court system. The litigated divorce process begins when one spouse (in legal terms, the *plaintiff* or the *petitioner*) files a complaint (sometimes called a *petition*) for divorce with the court. The other spouse (the *defendant* or *respondent*) will be served divorce papers by a constable, a sheriff, or someone else with the authority to serve legal documents. From that point, the defendant has a specified number of days to respond to the complaint. A divorce response, like a divorce complaint, is a legal document. The response serves as both an acknowledgment of receipt of the divorce complaint and an opportunity for the defendant to formally agree or disagree with the information, issues, and requests included in the complaint. Your spouse may ask for support in their petition; you may disagree with that request. Your spouse may file a fault divorce, citing fault reasons you don't think are valid. Your spouse may ask for full legal or physical custody of your children; you may object to this. If your spouse is the one to file a complaint, you can state your disagreements in your response.

Each state has its own rules and guidelines for the process of litigating divorces, but typically what follows is a series of scheduled hearings with the court to check in on the progress being made in negotiation. If necessary, the court will make interim decisions on key issues in your case, often related to your children (to resolve issues such as temporary child support, parenting time, vacation plans, and medical decisions) or your home (who will pay the mortgage, taxes, maintenance, and other expenses during your divorce).

The court will also oversee *discovery*, the process used in litigation to gather and share information between parties, including all financial information. Once negotiation has resolved the issues in your case, a settlement agreement will be drafted, signed, and presented to the court for review, along with each spouse's financial statement. You and your spouse will go to court and appear in front of a judge, who will ask you questions to ensure that the agreement has been arrived at fairly and equitably. You and your spouse will be asked to confirm that you have had an opportunity to have your legal counsel review the agreement and that you understand what you have signed and how you are expected to perform to abide by your agreement.

If you and your spouse cannot resolve your financial and custody issues through negotiation, your case will go to trial in front of a judge, who will consider the evidence in your case and make rulings to resolve any unresolved issues, including parenting time and responsibility, spousal and child support, and division of marital property (your assets and debts).

WHAT ROLES DO PROFESSIONALS PLAY IN LITIGATION?

The judge plays a decisive, controlling role in a litigated divorce. The judge oversees the entire process, makes rulings to resolve interim disputes and issues temporary orders to address improper behavior, sets timelines and deadlines for the resolution of the case, sets a trial date when issues aren't resolved, makes decisions at the conclusion of the trial to settle your case, and reviews final settlement and custody agreements in cases that have settled without going to trial. Attorneys also play a significant role in litigated divorces, representing parties in court hearings, filing motions, using the formal discovery process to get financial information, negotiating on their clients' behalf, and presenting clients' cases at trial. Depending on the circumstances of your case, a judge may appoint other professionals, which can include:

- *Guardians ad litem*, professionals appointed by the court to represent the best interests of minor children.

- *Discovery masters*, attorneys appointed by the court to assist with the discovery process. (Clients, through their attorneys, may also be able to request that discovery masters be added to their case.)

- *Parenting coordinators*, neutral third parties who help divorcing parents communicate effectively about their children and resolve parenting issues in a divorce, such as parenting time, division of parenting responsibilities, and development of a parenting schedule. (Clients, through their attorneys, may also be able to request that parenting coordinators be added to their case.)

HOW IS FINANCIAL INFORMATION ACQUIRED IN LITIGATION?

In litigation, as in all methods of case resolution, each spouse is expected to be forthcoming about their finances. In a litigated divorce, disclosure of financial information between spouses is mandated. The formal process of discovery is used to acquire financial information that is not supplied fully and accurately through the initial, mandated disclosure requirements. Attorneys file *motions*—requests filed with the court to mandate a certain action—to produce financial documents and other information. A hearing on the motion will take place in court and a judge will decide what action is to be taken. The discovery process employs several tools to retrieve information related to your case:

- *Interrogatories* are formal sets of questions issued from one spouse to another, seeking information and clarification about a spouse's financial position. The recipient must answer all questions in writing within a specified period.

- *Subpoenas* can be issued to third parties, such as business part- ners, employers, banks, places of employment, and credit card companies. The person or institution that receives a subpoena must comply with the request and produce the requested docu- ments or information within a specified period.

- *Witnesses* can be ordered to participate in *depositions*—answering questions from lawyers under oath, outside of court—to provide financial information. Witnesses can also be called to testify in court if your case goes to trial.

WHAT ARE THE PROS AND CONS OF LITIGATION?

Litigation is the first method we're discussing here, but in practice, it should be your last choice as a process for resolving your divorce. Litiga- tion is expensive, intrusive, and stressful; tends to generate animosity between spouses; and abdicates control over your case to the judge.

That said, litigation is an essential process for resolving divorces when spouses cannot agree on how to settle their case. And using the court to litigate a divorce offers powerful legal tools that are necessary in some cases. Courts have the power to activate legal guardrails and enforce compliance. Temporary and emergency orders issued by the court are used to address a number of circumstances, including to estab- lish interim spousal and child support, to prevent spouses from selling or transferring marital assets, and to require spouses to pay their share of marital expenses and debts while a divorce is ongoing. (Temporary orders are also used to establish interim parenting schedules for minor children.) The mandated, formal discovery process and the power to sub- poena information and witnesses make it possible to get accurate and complete financial information from a spouse who has failed to report assets or income, or who is hiding or de-valuing assets. Litigation is often your best recourse when dealing with a narcissistic spouse or a spouse who tries to control the negotiation process. Nobody wants to go to trial. The possibility of having a judge decide the terms of a settlement may be the only thing that makes a domineering, combative spouse willing to compromise and agree to a settlement in negotiation.

As in all forms of case resolution, cooperation between spouses has an impact on how long it will take to finalize a litigated divorce, and how much the process will cost. (When you use litigation, the time frame for resolving your case is also dependent on the court's schedule.) The more cooperative the parties are, the faster and less expensive the process will be.

The expense, delays, and animosity of litigation often arise from prolonged and extensive discovery. Extended and extensive discovery can happen for a number of reasons, including:

- One spouse attempts to hide or withhold money or information. This leads the other party to subpoena information, often from the spouse's employer or business, usually to the embarrassment and anger of the spouse.

- Spouses cannot agree on the value of marital assets, or one spouse attempts to devalue assets, whether by spending them or by presenting a low valuation, leading to new rounds of valuation and/or additional discovery to document improper spending.

🔥 *Red Flag* Valuation of assets (homes and commercial real estate, a privately held business, art, cars, jewelry, watches, wine) is something of an art, rather than a science, and often leads to protracted, expensive litigation when spouses can't agree and additional valuations are ordered. Valuation of a business is particularly sensitive for the spouse who founded the business. Having a third-party valuation expert examine the books and question business expenses gets under people's skin and can create animosity. However, it may be a necessary task to ensure that you are getting an accurate value of the marital estate.

✖ **DON'T** hesitate to require that potentially high-value assets be professionally appraised if they are subject to division in your divorce. If the assets are to be sold in a transaction on the open market and the proceeds divided, then you may not need a valuation, since the fair-market value will prevail.

IS LITIGATION RIGHT FOR ME?

If you can be cooperative with your spouse, and if you and your spouse can come to an agreement on the value of the finances to be divided in your divorce, then stay away from litigation. If you don't agree with what your spouse is reporting in their financial statement, and if, after third-party valuations, you still can't agree on valuations of a business or other assets, or if your spouse is withholding money from you or spending marital assets, then you may have no choice but to litigate.

Keep in mind, you can litigate certain issues and not your entire divorce. For example, if you can't get complete financial information from your spouse, you can subpoena that information and then return to mediation. You can use the litigation process to obtain financial information and settle financial disputes and use mediation to settle custody and other matters related to your children.

Using Mediation to Divorce

Mediation is a method of alternative dispute resolution (ADR) that takes place outside of the court system. Guided by a trained mediator, spouses work directly with each other to resolve their issues and reach a settlement in their divorce. Mediation gives divorcing spouses control over the decision-making in their divorce and relies on cooperation, direct communication, and problem-solving between spouses to come to a final agreement. Mediation offers you and your spouse the opportunity to decide how you will divide marital property, come to agreement about spousal and child support, and make decisions about parenting time and responsibilities, based on what works for your family.

You do not need to file a divorce complaint with the court to begin mediation. You and your spouse may hire a mediator yourselves. Discussions in mediation are confidential. Financial documents shared in mediation are not confidential and can be used in litigation or another process if mediation doesn't resolve your case. Child-related matters, such as parenting time, are often the first topic addressed in mediation, while spouses work to compile their financial information. Mediation sessions typically happen every two weeks and continue until the parties have negotiated through all the financial and child- and family-related components of their settlement.

When issues of disagreement arise between you and your spouse, the mediator may offer suggestions for an equitable solution, but they will not advocate for either one of you. It's important to meet with your attorney between mediation sessions so they can advise you on negotiating the components of your agreement and review decisions you're making in mediation sessions. When you and your spouse have worked through all the issues in your case, the mediator will create a *memorandum of understanding*, which outlines the proposed financial agreement and parenting agreement. Your attorney will review it to ensure it treats you fairly, make sure that you understand the terms you have agreed to, and then work with you to draft a final financial settlement, parenting agreement, and divorce agreement. A final agreement will be submitted to the court for review and approval by a judge.

WHAT ROLES DO PROFESSIONALS PLAY IN MEDIATION?

A mediator facilitates the process through which spouses negotiate and resolve the issues in their divorce. Mediators do not give legal advice, and not all mediators are lawyers. They do not take sides in a case. They do not decide how issues in your case should be—or will be—resolved. The mediator establishes the rules for the negotiation process, creates an agenda for mediation sessions, and helps spouses communicate constructively and stay focused on problem-solving and finding common-ground solutions for their disputes. Attorneys are sometimes present during mediation sessions. More often, spouses attend mediation sessions without their attorneys, and consult with their attorneys between mediation meetings. Remember, not all lawyers are mediators and not all mediators are lawyers.

> ✔ **DO** have your lawyer review the draft agreement as it develops throughout mediation. That way, the proposed settlement you've worked hard to negotiate isn't deemed unfair by your lawyer at the end of the process, creating stress and adding time and expense to the process when you would otherwise be wrapping up.

HOW IS FINANCIAL INFORMATION ACQUIRED AND HANDLED IN MEDIATION?

In mediation, financial information is provided voluntarily. The discovery process is not used in mediation, because it is understood that the parties are coming to the table willingly and are prepared to be fully forthcoming in their financial disclosures. There is no subpoena power available in mediation. To file a subpoena or use other tools of discovery, a divorce complaint must be filed with the court.

WHAT ARE THE PROS AND CONS OF MEDIATION?

When it works, the mediation process is a superb option for speed, efficiency, and cost. If both parties are willing to cooperate and work through their issues calmly with a business mindset, the process can move relatively quickly to reach a final agreement. You and your spouse will provide each other with the required financial information and order valuations of your marital assets (home, collections, investments, and other property). You can come to agreement about division of your assets and debts and use state calculators to determine child support and spousal support. Successful mediation typically requires significantly less lawyer time than litigation, which lowers the cost of divorce, even after adding the expense of a mediator. Mediated divorce agreements are a little like real estate deals—considered successful when both parties are a little unhappy.

Mediation is inherently cooperative; successful mediation requires spouses to listen to each other and work together to reconfigure their finances and their family life. Mediation can help you maintain a positive relationship with your ex-spouse after your divorce is final. The reduced conflict and stress between spouses also can make mediation beneficial for your children's emotional well-being, and help both parents maintain more positive relationships with their children.

If mediation doesn't work, you will need to file a divorce complaint with the court and start a new process with your lawyer. Depending where and why mediation failed, you may have to renegotiate issues you settled in that forum. This time, your attorneys will likely negotiate for you and your spouse. If information gathered through the mediation process is not complete and accurate, you and/or your spouse will need to use the discovery process to request information, subpoena records, and possibly order new valuations.

IS MEDIATION RIGHT FOR MY CASE?

There is a lot of trust that goes into the mediation process. In mediation, you don't have the power of court-mandated discovery. If you don't trust your spouse to provide complete and accurate financial information, this process may not be the right option for you. Some spouses seek out mediation because they think that they can control the process, the information, and the outcome. A family dynamic in which one spouse bullies or overpowers the other will carry into the mediation process, creating a significant disadvantage to the "weaker" spouse, and the mediator, as a neutral third party, has limited power to address these dynamics. If you are married to a narcissist, mediation won't work. Manipulation, a need for control, a lack of consideration for others, an outsized sense of entitlement: the traits of a narcissist are at odds with the process of mediation. If your spouse is hiding information or assets, and/or attempting to control the process, mediation is not the right approach for you.

In order to decide on the right divorce process, Vita and Taylor met with several family law lawyers and mediators who were recommended by their financial advisors and their friends. Taylor moved to an apartment in the same town so they could continue to coparent. The couple didn't file right away and felt they could work out most of their issues, but they needed guidance. As a result of their cooperative approach to their children and households, they decided that mediation was the best way to begin.

Together, Vita and Taylor met with Karla, an attorney-mediator, who laid out the process. They would meet at Karla's office every two weeks for a two-hour session. Karla would be paid at the end of every session at her regular billable hour rate and a check would be written from the spouses' joint checking account.

Before the first session, Vita and Taylor completed the financial statements required by their state of residence. These financial statements would be updated and exchanged periodically so Vita and Taylor could review each other's income, expenses, savings, and debts.

The first issue to resolve was a consistent, reliable parenting plan for the children. Which nights were they to spend with Vita, and which with Taylor? Where would they spend weekends, school holidays, birthdays, and religious events? What would happen if Taylor had an unexpected business trip? Who would take the kids to medical checkups, the dentist, and therapy? What percentage of time would the children be with each parent?

Next, Vita and Taylor will discuss how they plan to financially support their children. Karla (and their lawyers and financial advisors) will review the couple's pay stubs, W-2s, and 1099s as well as three years of tax returns to determine income in order to calculate child support using the state's formula. Karla will provide the support numbers and discuss the couple's options for making the payments, coming to agreement about what the support will cover (food, clothing, and shelter at the very least) and what will happen if a significant change were to occur with either party's income or expenses—a point of significant interest for Vita, who hoped to build her graphic design business in the years to come.

Next on the agenda will likely be alimony. Karla will discuss the law, explain the state's eligibility guidelines, and facilitate a conversation between Vita and Taylor to decide if, how much, and for how long spousal support would be paid.

After Karla, Taylor and Vita, their attorneys, and their financial advisors all review the spouses' financial statements and supporting documents from financial institutions, Karla will facilitate a discussion about dividing the marital assets and debts according to the laws in their state of residence.

At this point, Karla will walk the couple through the remaining issues to be worked out: health insurance for the kids; life insurance for both parents to cover the financial obligation if either dies before the children are emancipated; a plan to share in extraordinary expenses such as orthodontia, overnight summer camps, religious celebrations (e.g., bar/bat mitzvahs), drivers' education, and tutoring; and—a major priority for both parents—a plan for how to fund their children's college. Vita and Taylor started 529 college savings plans when the kids were born. They continued to make contributions to the accounts and had built up a decent savings, and both were hoping to continue to regularly contribute to these accounts after the divorce, but they weren't sure what they'd be able to afford. They also didn't know whether their 529s would cover the full cost of college when the time comes (their young children were four and six). They can decide to create a plan to contribute to the 529s to the best of their ability for the foreseeable future, or agree to take out parental loans (PLUS), have the kids take out loans, and apply for state and federal aid (FAFSA). They can also agree to deal with this issue when the children are older and they have a better sense of where the children may attend and what the financial gap between the 529 savings and the actual costs will be.

If Vita and Taylor can come to an agreement on their issues, Karla will draft a memorandum of understanding between the parties that reflects their agreement and terms. Vita and Taylor will each take the draft agreement to their independent attorney for review. Once the independent attorneys have signed off on the agreement, a final agreement will be drafted and filed with the court for a hearing date and approval. At this point, Karla's role in their divorce will end. Vita and Taylor will proceed to court (with their respective attorneys if they wish, but this is typically not mandatory) and appear in front of a judge. The judge may ask questions about the agreement, whether Vita and Taylor understand what they are agreeing to via the agreement, and if they have each had an opportunity to consult with an attorney. In some cases the judge may raise an issue of concern and return the agreement for clarity or revision. However, if Vita, Taylor, Karla, and the independent attorneys have been honest, forthcoming, and transparent, the judge will accept the agreement as drafted and enter a final judgment of divorce.

Using Arbitration to Divorce

Arbitration is a private proceeding that takes place in front of a private judge or arbitrator. You and your spouse will hire an arbitrator (often a former judge or attorney) to make decisions about your case. The decision to take your case to arbitration must be approved by a judge in the family court where your case has been filed. Your attorney will present your case in a hearing, after which the arbitrator will issue a ruling.

The most significant difference between arbitration and other paths to divorce is that the private judge's decision is binding and, under most circumstances, cannot be changed or appealed to a higher court. This can work to your advantage if your spouse is particularly litigious, as it stops them from running back to court on the issue, but it also removes the possibility of rearguing your case if you feel that the judge misunderstood or misinterpreted critical information.

★ *Gabrielle's Pro Tip* Some states allow arbitration in divorce to settle financial issues only, and do not allow arbitration to be used for custody or child-related matters. Other states allow arbitration for all disputes in a divorce, including financial issues and matters related to children. Arbitration is best suited to resolving complex financial issues that don't impact people's changing circumstances over time. To resolve disagreements about children or nonfinancial family matters, it would be best to use a different process.

WHAT ROLES DO PROFESSIONALS PLAY IN ARBITRATION?

You and your spouse decide which issues you want an arbitrator to decide. The arbitrator, who is often a former family court judge or a former divorce lawyer, has the final say over the issues you present to them, and you typically have no opportunity to appeal. Arbitrators have areas of expertise, not only specific to divorce but also with resolving certain types of financial disputes, such as those over property or business interests. Usually, both parties' attorneys are involved in identifying an arbitrator who is a right fit for your case. Your attorney will present evidence and make legal arguments to support your case in your arbitration hearing and may call witnesses to testify and submit documents into evidence.

HOW IS FINANCIAL INFORMATION ACQUIRED AND HANDLED IN ARBITRATION?

The specific rules and process for sharing information and documents is determined by the arbitrator in your case, who will oversee the exchange of information to make sure you and your spouse are complying with the rules. Financial documents may be shared voluntarily between spouses, but full disclosure of all financial information is expected and ultimately mandatory.

WHAT ARE THE PROS AND CONS OF ARBITRATION?

Compared to a court trial, an arbitration hearing will typically be heard sooner, proceed more efficiently, and cost less. Unlike in litigation, where your hearings and trial will be scheduled by the court, you and your spouse will schedule your arbitration hearing, and as a result, you're likely to have your case heard more quickly. Arbitration hearings are similar to court hearings, but their process is more informal. Arbitration, unlike litigation, allows parties to state their case in a confidential setting. (Your court records will still be public.) Arbitration is a more focused, streamlined process for resolving disputes, and as a result, will typically cost less than litigation.

That said, using an arbitrator to resolve your case can be risky business. On one hand, you can move through the divorce process faster, cheaper, and more efficiently, but on the other, you are likely giving up the valuable opportunity to appeal the arbitrator's decision to a higher court and have it reviewed for error if you don't like or agree with it. In essence, you're stuck with the decision whether you like it or not.

IS ARBITRATION RIGHT FOR MY CASE?

The divorce process is stressful and uncomfortable, particularly when you use litigation, which may make the streamlined, somewhat expedited process of arbitration appealing for spouses who can't come to an agreement themselves. That said, it may be to your advantage to retain the option to have your case reviewed by a higher court if the family court judge in your case makes decisions you don't agree with. If you're going in front of a judge—whether a private judge in arbitration or a judge in family court—that means you and your spouse disagree about certain facts or circumstances in your case, and you need a judge to resolve the issue. Ask yourself, *What is the rush?*

If the dispute in your case is a complex financial matter, or one that has a small bearing on your case, consider carefully the impact of getting an adverse decision. *How will you feel if the ruling doesn't go your way? What are the consequences for you if the arbitrator rules against you? What is the worst that can happen from this outcome?* If you are prepared to live with the answers, then move forward with arbitration. If not, reconsider arbitration as a process for your case.

Remember, throughout the course of your case, you can remove specific issues of conflict and resolve them outside of your primary process. I worked with a couple who were using mediation to settle their divorce and ran into a sticking point over a private, closely held company that one spouse founded during their marriage. Each spouse hired a business valuation expert to appraise the business, and the two experts came back with values that were leagues apart. My client and their spouse were unable to compromise, so they took the matter to an arbitrator who heard their case, reviewed the appraisals, and made a final decision that couldn't be appealed. My client and their spouse took that decision back to mediation and moved on to settle the rest of the financial issues in their divorce.

Using Collaborative Law to Divorce

Collaborative law takes a highly cooperative, team-based approach to negotiation and settlement in a divorce. In this process, spouses agree to work on the same team to come to an agreement in their divorce. Each spouse hires an attorney trained in the collaborative law process and meets with their attorney individually in an initial meeting. Spouses then take the lead in negotiating their agreement, with their lawyers and other team members present to assist them.

Before negotiations begin, spouses, their attorneys, and the other collaborative-law-trained professionals all sign a participation agreement, which lays out the rules by which everyone will abide. A participation agreement includes a commitment by the parties to negotiate honestly and respectfully, to be fully transparent in sharing all information related to the case (including all financial information), and to keep confidential the information shared in the collaborative process. *In a participation agreement, spouses agree not to go to court to resolve their divorce.* Spouses, their lawyers, and the rest of the professional team agree, in writing, that if the collaborative process doesn't work to reach a final settlement, all professionals will withdraw from the case and spouses will hire new attorneys and other professionals to advise them, as they take their case to another method of resolution.

WHAT ROLES DO PROFESSIONALS PLAY IN COLLABORATIVE LAW?

If you choose this route, you will work with attorneys and other professionals who are formally trained in the collaborative law process. A collaborative law divorce often includes several professionals playing active, supporting roles in negotiations, including divorce coaches, therapists, and parenting coordinators. Depending on the collaborative law guidelines in the state where your case resides, you may have the option to hire a single divorce coach to work with both you and your spouse, or to each hire your own divorce coach to support you through the process.

Collaborative law also uses a *financial neutral*—a financial expert trained in collaborative law who will work on behalf of both parties— to help spouses document their financial information, suggest ways to structure a financial settlement, and work with spouses to budget and plan for their financial lives after divorce.

This entire team of professionals is present during negotiations and can help spouses communicate and work through conflicts, assist in developing parenting plans, and offer suggestions for compromise in any area of the settlement. In the collaborative process, the parties speak for themselves, while the lawyers and other professionals stand back and allow the parties to express their desired outcome. If there are conflicts, coaches and therapists or financial neutrals can weigh in with suggestions.

HOW IS FINANCIAL INFORMATION ACQUIRED AND HANDLED IN COLLABORATIVE LAW?

Financial information is provided voluntarily. The collaborative process relies on spouses to be fully forthcoming with each other about their finances.

WHAT ARE THE PROS AND CONS OF COLLABORATIVE LAW?

The collaborative process gives divorcing spouses a lot of control and ownership of the process. At the same time, it offers a great deal of guidance and support, with a robust team of professionals, all trained in the process, present in negotiations. Lawyers, coaches and coordinators, therapists, and neutral financial advisors are all working to help spouses reach a settlement that works best for their family. When it works, collaborative law often yields a final settlement that both spouses can feel comfortable and at peace with, and spouses often feel a sense of shared ownership over the outcome they worked actively and cooperatively to achieve.

Collaborative law may be less expensive than litigation, but it's likely to be more expensive than mediation because it engages more paid professionals: divorce coach, therapist, financial neutral, as well as attorneys. In the collaborative process, you don't have access to the powerful tools of the court without abandoning the process and starting over with new attorneys. You don't have subpoena power or the power to ask the courts to issue mandated orders; you rely on trust that your spouse is acting honorably and that you are receiving the best and most complete financial information. That is a big leap in divorce, where self-preservation is paramount.

IS COLLABORATIVE LAW RIGHT FOR MY CASE?

The collaborative law process can work if you and your spouse are in complete agreement about the scope and value of your marital assets and liabilities and are able to be highly cooperative in deciding the terms of your divorce settlement. You must also feel very comfortable speaking for yourself. Under these circumstances, collaborative law may be a right fit for you.

Be sure you understand what you are getting into here. Using collaborative law is expensive and time-consuming, and the failure rate is very high. Do your research and be honest with yourself about whether you trust your spouse to come to the table with all the required information. If the process breaks down, you are prohibited from using any of the professionals involved in your collaborative case. That's an expensive restart, one that adds significant time to the duration of your case.

★ *Gabrielle's Pro Tip*   The cooperative team approach is formalized in collaborative law—but you can decide to employ both the spirit and some of the methods of this approach no matter what case resolution method you use. You and your spouse can commit to communicating respectfully and to being honest in your disclosures and discussions. You each can create your own team of professionals to work together to support and advise you through your divorce. (Review my guidance for helping teams collaborate successfully in Chapter 1.) You and your spouse can hire divorce attorneys who will zealously represent each of your interests and simultaneously focus on negotiating a fair settlement without ratcheting up adversarial tension and conflict. This approach will get you through your divorce more quickly, will keep your costs down, and will spare you and your family the stress and emotional toll of a high-conflict divorce.

How to Find a Lawyer

Choosing a divorce lawyer is a very personal decision. It is one of the most important decisions you'll make in your divorce. And it's one of the steps that, for many people, leads to the most anxiety. There is no one-size-fits-all formula for choosing a lawyer to handle your divorce. You need an attorney who is a right fit for your case. What does that mean exactly? A right-fit attorney for *you* is:

AN ATTORNEY WHO HAS TIME FOR YOU. The best attorney will be of little help if they turn around and delegate your case to an associate, junior attorney. (And you'll be paying for all of them.) You need an attorney who has the time in their schedule to be engaged with your case from start to finish.

AN ATTORNEY WHO UNDERSTANDS YOUR CASE. You want a lawyer with experience, and one who focuses their practice on divorce and family law. Your attorney should have experience handling cases similar to yours. For example, if your divorce involves complicated financial issues, you want an attorney who has successfully handled financially complex divorces in the past, and is comfortable and open to working with your financial advisor. Your lawyer should take the time to learn about you, your marriage, and your goals and expectations in your divorce.

AN ATTORNEY WHO IS WILLING TO WORK WITH OTHER MEMBERS OF YOUR TEAM. A good attorney will not object to having a team (a CPA, a qualified divorce financial advisor, a divorce coach, etc.) in place. The attitude you're looking for here is "the more, the merrier" if it will help you, the client, move through the process efficiently, confidently, and with less stress and confusion. However, no one wants to feel they are in competition with the other advisors. Remember to conduct a team meeting to ensure that everyone is on the same page, strategically, legally, ethically, and morally.

AN ATTORNEY WHOSE APPROACH ALIGNS WITH YOURS. If you want a civil, cooperative divorce, you need an attorney who is willing to work civilly and cooperatively, while zealously advocating for you. If you want to avoid a trial, you need an attorney who is skilled and effective at negotiating. To achieve your goals, you need a lawyer who understands them and is prepared to communicate with you honestly and transparently about whether they are realistic—and help you set new ones, in line with your priorities and values, if they are not.

AN ATTORNEY YOU FEEL COMFORTABLE WORKING WITH. You need to feel that you can trust your attorney to handle your case. Your attorney should communicate with you honestly and respectfully; take the time to educate you about the legal process; answer questions about your case; keep you informed of all meetings, hearings, and developments; and help you set—and maintain—reasonable expectations for the outcome in your divorce. You need to feel comfortable sharing personal information with your lawyer.

> ✔ **DO** be honest and forthcoming with your attorney as you answer their questions about your marriage, your family, and your finances. Tell them everything, but also be sure to ask if they are mandatory reporters if you have something sensitive to share.

When looking for an attorney, consider:

THEIR EXPERIENCE

Nothing beats experience. You want to work with an attorney who has made divorce their professional focus. When you are interviewing prospective attorneys, you may already know which method you and your spouse are likely to use to resolve your case, or you may not. Regardless, look for an attorney with expertise in different case resolution methods. (Remember, you may start out with one approach but need to switch to another to resolve all or parts of your case.) The relationships your lawyer has with other professionals in your case—the judge, the clerks in your local courthouse, your spouse's attorney—will have a huge impact on how effectively they can work your case and get you the most favorable outcome possible in a settlement.

Ask:

- *How many years have you practiced family/divorce law?*

- *How much of your practice is focused on divorce cases?*

- *How many divorces have you handled? How many of your cases have gone to trial versus settling out of court?*

- *Have you handled cases similar to mine? What was your approach in resolving those cases?*

- *What are your thoughts about and experience in mediation? Arbitration? Collaborative law?* (To use the collaborative process, you and your spouse will both need to hire an attorney who has been specifically trained in collaborative law.)

- *What method do you think best suits my case?*

- *What is your experience with the judge in my case?*

- *Have you appeared in front of my judge?*

- *How often do you work in my county's courthouse?*

- *Do you know the clerks?*

- *Have you worked with my spouse's attorney?*
- *If so, what is your impression of that attorney? Are you comfortable working with them?*

★ *Gabrielle's Pro Tip* Your lawyer's reputation with the judge transcends your case. Your lawyer may be in front of that judge ten times in a week, and their credibility with the judge is critical to their effectiveness as a lawyer. Be aware, this reputational consideration works in both directions: unless there are valid extenuating circumstances, your lawyer will not want to lose face in front of the judge by making unreasonable requests to help you get more or pay less if these requests are out of step with your state's divorce laws and guidelines.

THEIR ACCESSIBILITY

I can't stress enough how important it is to make sure your lawyer has the time in their schedule to devote to your case. You're hiring an attorney for their experience, their relationships with the court, and their expertise in negotiating settlements in cases like yours. When your attorney passes your case off to an associate, you're no longer working with the person you hired. Make sure your attorney is committed and available to do the legwork on your case.

🔥 *Red Flag* Attorneys show their value to their firms through their billable hours, and also through their origination of new cases—the number of cases they bring into their firm. Unfortunately, some lawyers working their way up in their firm may take on more cases than they can handle to raise their origination numbers, having calculated that it's worth it to their standing in the firm to bring the case in, even if they don't keep it in the end when the client leaves dissatisfied.

Ask:

- *Do you have time for my case?*
- *What is your caseload?*

- *Will I be working with you directly or will you assign my case to a junior associate?*

- *Will there be more than one attorney on my case? A junior attorney?*

- *If my case ultimately needs to go to trial, will you be the attorney to argue my case in court?*

- *How will we communicate? How can I get in touch with you?*

- *How quickly do you return phone calls?*

THEIR APPROACH

You are looking for a legal advocate who will work zealously on your behalf—and that includes seeking out a fair compromise wherever it is possible and in your best interests. Steer clear of the lawyer who tells you they are going to "take your ex to the cleaners." That just doesn't happen. This is bad advice that runs completely counter to setting realistic expectations in your divorce. And beware the lawyer who promises big results right from the start. It takes time for your attorney to get fully up to speed on the facts and circumstances in your case. And remember, in most cases, a realistic outcome is a 50-50 split of marital property, or something close to it.

You want a lawyer who is focused on developing a sound legal strategy and problem-solving along the way to a settlement. Don't be taken in by lots of negative and aggressive talk that bashes your spouse or their attorney. That's nothing more than hot air that inflames tension and negative, adversarial emotions—and ultimately will cost you time and money, when your lawyer can't deliver an effective approach to negotiations. You're working hard to keep your emotions out of the business of your divorce. You need a lawyer who shares your goal of keeping things civil, calm, professional, and focused on getting you the best possible settlement.

Pay attention to how prospective lawyers communicate with you. You need a lawyer who listens carefully and takes the time to educate and advise you on the law and the legal prospects for your case. You need a lawyer to be honest with you and help you identify realistic outcomes for your case. It's important that you feel your lawyer understands you. They may not always be able to get you exactly what you want, but in the end, you want to feel that you were understood, heard, and valued as a person.

Ask yourself:

- *Do I feel listened to and heard? Is this person engaged and focused on me?*

- *Does this attorney ask follow-up questions?*

- *Are they interrupting me mid-sentence? Do they talk over me?*

- *Do they speak to me respectfully?*

- *Are they taking the time to fully address my questions?*

- *Do I feel that this person will understand and respect my culture, traditions, and values?*

- *Can I imagine sharing personal information with this person?* (You will likely need to share details of your marriage, your personal history, and your finances with your attorney.)

Ask the attorney:

- *Can you reiterate for me what you understand to be the issues in my case, and my goals for the outcome of my divorce?*

- *What do you see as the strengths and weaknesses in my case?*

- *Are my goals for resolving my case reasonable?*

- *How do you envision your approach to my case?*

- *Can I have my client file when we are done?*

> ✔ **DO** trust your gut. If a prospective attorney is abrupt with you, seems distracted or too busy for you, or just doesn't feel right, listen to your instincts and move on.

THEIR BILLING PRACTICES

Most lawyers charge by the hour, and most will expect a *retainer*—an upfront payment that will cover a portion of their services. Attorneys bill for partial hours in increments, often fifteen minutes, even if they only do a few minutes of work. And there are separate hourly fees for junior attorneys and paralegals who contribute to your case. Be sure you understand all this information up front, so you know what to expect. Speak up and ask questions about anything you don't understand. You should expect to receive an itemized description of all work done on your case with every bill.

Ask:

- *How do you bill?*
- *How much do you charge? What is the hourly fee for an associate on my case? The hourly fee for paralegal work?*
- *Do you require a retainer up front?*
- *If we stop working together, will I still need to pay your full fee?*
- *Will I receive itemized bills?*
- *If you are in the courthouse hallway waiting to be called for a hearing in my case, are you billing other clients as you fill the time working on their case and also billing me?*
- *Do you charge for photocopies?*
- *What other expenses do you bill for outside of your hourly rate?*
- *What is the process if we have a dispute about my bill?*

> ✖ **DON'T** hire the lawyer who is the cheapest (*I'm getting a deal!*) or most expensive (*They must be the best!*). Pick the person with the experience, relationships, approach, and personality that are the best fit for you and your situation.

Margo and Chris weren't talking much, and when they did it was tense. But they were in agreement about one thing: they wanted to get their divorce done quickly, and with as little reliance on lawyers as possible. Chris was already complaining about the upcoming expenses, and Margo had heard horror stories about hard-charging lawyers. They decided to try mediation and muddled through the first couple of two-hour sessions without much progress. Margo was regularly updating her financial statements, and when she went online to get an updated value for the savings account, she was surprised to see that there had been a series of large and uncharacteristic ATM withdrawals from machines all over the city. Since she and Chris usually put everything on a credit card, they rarely used ATMs or cash at all. Margo hadn't received any bank statements recently because the address on the account had been changed to Chris's new residence. Margo looked back at the last few months of statements online and noticed that a significant amount of money had been moved out of their joint account through electronic transfers, cash withdrawals, and a cashier's check (money order). Her blood pressure rose as her heart sank. Chris was taking their money, *her* money—money earned and intended for their family, their children. How could he? When did this begin? Chris hadn't mentioned anything about the cash transfers, extra expenses, or new bank accounts in the mediation session.

Margo met with me to sort through and help her understand the last twelve months of bank records and credit card statements and prior three years of tax returns. Chris had not provided a new pay stub in months. Up until now, Margo hadn't been concerned about any financial activity because she and Chris had agreed to be honest and forthcoming in order to get the divorce over quickly, efficiently, and without using lawyers, who would be expensive and charge too much.

But the tides were changing. Chris was seeing less of the kids, and Margo heard Chris had been seen around town with a new "friend." Chris had stopped paying the full balance on their credit cards and switched to paying the minimum balances due, which meant their debt was increasing.

Margo gathered her reports, documents, and statements and headed into mediation prepared with her questions. When Chris realized that his financial activity had been discovered, he became defensive and argumentative and stormed out of mediation. Mediation is a process that requires full disclosure, and the mediator felt that Chris's intentions were no longer aligned with the spirit of the process. The mediator regretfully withdrew from the case.

It was back to the drawing board for Margo and Chris.

Margo met with a few family law attorneys and found their strategies, approach to the case, hourly rate, and general availability were very different. After thoughtful consideration, Margo chose Nancy, a no-nonsense lawyer who took the time to listen to her story, asked questions, and had time for her case. She paid Nancy a retainer, gave her the files from mediation, and went on her way.

"Chris Adams?" asked the stocky man at the door.

"Yes," replied Chris, expecting a UPS delivery, signature required.

"You've been served." The man pushed official-looking paperwork into his hands before turning and walking down the front steps.

"What is this?"

Upon being retained, Nancy filed a complaint for divorce in the county where Margo and Chris live. The complaint for divorce started the timeline on the divorce proceedings through the state court system. Timelines, status hearings, forms, financial statements, mandatory mediation, and response deadlines will all provide a framework for the case as it works its way through the family court system.

Upon receiving the complaint for divorce, Chris hired Brian, a high-profile, well-known family law shark attorney. Margo and Chris's case, which had begun in mediation, was now in litigation.

Key Takeaways and Next Steps

- There is no right or wrong process to use to obtain a divorce. The right process for your case depends on your individual circumstances. The most important factor is the level of cooperation and trust you and your spouse can maintain throughout the process.

- You may use more than one divorce process to resolve all the issues in your case and arrive at a final agreement.

- Your lawyer is your most important guide through the legal process. Take the time to talk with prospective divorce attorneys to find a lawyer with the approach and experience that suits you and your case. Your financial advisor can recommend attorneys based on their understanding of your case.

- Make sure your attorney has time to work on your case. Be sure you understand their billing practices right from the start.

PART TWO

DURING THE DIVORCE

CHAPTER FIVE

Not Together, Not Apart

Protecting Your Finances During Your Divorce

T his "limbo" stage—when you're no longer together as a married couple but not yet legally divorced—can be a confusing time. Your family is in crisis, undergoing profound change. The legal bills are starting to come in. Paying for two households is more expensive than one. Money is tight. Your family's lifestyle may no longer be affordable, and you're facing decisions about cutting expenses, finding new sources of income, whether to sell and downsize your family home. You're meeting with your lawyer, attending mediation sessions, or preparing to litigate. You and your spouse may be working collaboratively toward a final divorce agreement. No matter what route your divorce is taking, you have much important work to do. You and your spouse need to decide how you're going to pay your bills while your divorce is in progress. You need to create a budget to determine what you'll need to support your changing family. You must identify your needs and priorities for your financial settlement.

It's . . . a lot. It's no surprise if you feel at times like the puzzle you're trying to put together is a chaotic pile of pieces that will never fit.

As is so often the case in divorce, you have more control than you think. There are steps you can take right now to minimize conflict and delays, keep your divorce costs under control, and work toward a financial settlement that effectively addresses your financial needs. And whether your divorce is amicable or acrimonious, whether you plan to mediate or litigate, whether your marital assets are simple and straightforward or highly complex, there are basic steps every divorcing person should take during this phase to protect themselves financially.

Know Your Date of Separation

The date of your legal separation is a critical factor in your financial decision-making during your divorce. Every state treats legal separation differently. (See Chapter 1 to review the basics of legal separation and separation dates.) It is essential that you know what your state considers the date of legal separation. You also need to understand how that separation date affects your finances and your financial relationship with your spouse. Your date of separation may affect your legal liability for some debts your spouse generates before your divorce is final. It will affect the value of the assets you'll be dividing. It may affect your health insurance coverage during your divorce, if you're covered by your spouse's health insurance plan and the insurer or employer uses the date of separation, rather than the date of divorce, as the date to end coverage. Make it a top priority to discuss with your lawyer how legal separation works in your state, and make sure you understand how your separation date affects your specific financial circumstances.

Develop a Written Interim Financial Plan

Not all states recognize legal separation. But if your state of residence does recognize a legal separation period leading up to divorce, talk with your spouse and your attorney about drafting a formal, written, interim plan to establish how you'll handle financial matters. This interim plan can also include a parenting plan for the duration of your divorce. Your interim plan can outline how you and your spouse will care for and financially support your family, and establish parenting time and parenting responsibilities while your divorce is ongoing.

An interim plan can establish important contingency plans to protect you and your children financially. If you expect to receive spousal or child support, you may be able to use an interim plan to require your spouse to purchase a life insurance policy, naming you as the beneficiary.

An interim plan also can help you and your spouse address some important short-term estate planning issues until you're divorced. You and your spouse can agree, in writing, to make the financial arrangements of your interim plan binding for your agreed-upon heirs, so your children will receive the assets and income in the event one of you dies during your divorce. Some spouses choose to include a provision in an interim plan that waives their rights to a share of the other spouse's estate in the event of a death during the divorce period.

Maintain Your Family's Financial Status Quo

There is much that may change in your financial practices and arrangements during your divorce. But when it comes to routine family expenses, it is to your benefit to keep the status quo in place as much as possible. When a divorce complaint is filed, courts will automatically issue orders to keep the financial status quo in place, prohibiting spouses from transferring assets, spending excessively, or canceling insurance coverage. (That doesn't mean some spouses won't hide assets or spend inappropriately.) At some point—the sooner, the better—you and your spouse will need to agree on how you will pay joint household expenses during your divorce. You can do this the easy way, by coming to a voluntary arrangement to share income and expenses in keeping with the financial practices of your marriage and which enables both of you to pay the family bills and maintain your households. Or you can do it the hard way, with one spouse filing a motion with the court for temporary orders. Temporary orders will require the higher-earning spouse to pay a monthly payment of support during the divorce process to ensure that bills are covered and the basic needs of the family are met.

Keeping the financial status quo in place also means avoiding making large purchases or investments that are uncharacteristic for your family. Spending money on expensive "extras" can cause mistrust, give rise to accusations of marital dissipation, and bring scrutiny of your financial behavior from your spouse's legal team. That can lead to potential subpoenas, more legal fees, and additional time spent in divorce mode.

While your divorce is in progress, keep spending as simple and straightforward as you can. Keep your expenditures in line with how you spent money during your marriage, and don't spend money on things (or people) outside your marriage until your divorce is over. At that point, you will be free to move on and spend as you choose.

DEFINING "LEGITIMATE" SPENDING DURING A DIVORCE

Legitimate spending during a divorce is using marital funds to sustain your family and your households, consistent with how you and your spouse spent your shared funds during your marriage. Nothing more, nothing less. Overspending, spending on dating (hotels, restaurants, gifts, travel), or otherwise spending marital funds in ways that do not benefit your family could be construed as marital dissipation and you may have to repay the other spouse for half of those dollars spent.

If you're concerned your spouse is dissipating marital assets, keep records of the questionable spending and take contemporaneous notes on their financial behaviors. With those detailed records, you may be able to recoup the funds at the end of the divorce through an unequal distribution of marital assets. Inform your attorney and financial advisor as soon as you discover excessive spending so that your spouse is put on notice that you are watching and expect to be reimbursed. If you bring an accusation of marital dissipation to the court, it typically will be incumbent upon you to prove the improper spending. If you are successful, you may be reimbursed for half of the spent assets, since the other half of those assets belonged to your spouse. This generally happens at the end of the divorce as part of the settlement, in what is often referred to as a "true-up" to account for one spouse's excessive or otherwise illegitimate spending.

Being organized and informed is your best defense and offense around accusations of improper spending. While your divorce is in progress, don't make large, unusual, or otherwise extraordinary purchases that wouldn't have taken place during the marriage. Keep detailed and consistent records of your income and your expenses, and whenever possible, support your expenses with third-party documentation (e.g., receipts, bank and credit card statements, hotel bills, and airline tickets).

UNDERSTANDING TEMPORARY ORDERS

Whether because of a desire for revenge or control, the painful pinch of tight cash flow, or some combination of the above, one spouse may cut off income or access to marital assets from the other, rather than maintaining the family's status quo. Your spouse may suddenly redirect their paycheck to an unknown account and contribute only a fraction of what's historically been needed to keep the family afloat. If this happens, you can petition the court to order your spouse to provide temporary support to sustain your family as you work through your divorce and until a permanent agreement is put in place.

Temporary orders are an essential guardrail in the divorce process to maintain the family's financial status quo until a final settlement is reached. These orders can have consequences down the road in your divorce. The numbers always tell a story, and temporary orders serve as a preview to the court of what level of support is necessary and sufficient for spouses' post-divorce life. The dollar figures in temporary orders can often become the numbers in a final, court-approved agreement—and that can be a positive or negative outcome for either the support payor or the payee, depending on the circumstances. If you are the paying spouse, temporary support orders can result in greater support obligations than if you had voluntarily maintained the status quo in contributing income to your family.

If you are the recipient of temporary support and it can be shown that you can live comfortably on the amount of temporary support being provided, that gives weight to the argument that you don't need more support in your final agreement. (Remember, spousal support is based on the recipient's need and paying spouse's ability to pay.)

If you are receiving support through temporary orders and it's not enough, how are you closing the gap? Borrowing on credit cards? Spending down assets? Taking taxable distributions from your retirement accounts? Working more hours? Contributing less to retirement accounts? Reducing your tax withholdings on your income? Every one of these financial actions has consequences for your settlement and your long-term financial stability and should be discussed with your financial advisor and your attorney. If your lawyer can show that temporary support is not sufficient, you may be able to negotiate for or have a judge order additional support, at least for a period as you work through the financial transition of your divorce by reducing expenses and/or increasing income.

Communicating mostly through their lawyers, Margo and Chris set up a temporary parenting schedule and took inventory of their marital estate. The parenting schedule they agreed to calmed the waters between them a bit, and it gave both the spouses and their children some much-needed routine and structure amid the emotional upheaval and crisis taking place in their family. Margo was hopeful that the move out of mediation and into litigation would help them stay on track. She felt she needed the unwelcome, expensive prospect of a court trial to keep Chris in line. Her hopes faded upon reviewing Chris's financial disclosure. Margo saw that Chris had failed to report his individual bank account. The next day, Margo received a call from a credit card company where she didn't have an account, asking for verification of a recent, large purchase. Margo began to suspect that Chris was spending their marital funds on people and activity outside of the marriage. She took out their recent credit card statements and gave them a close review, making note of charges for expensive restaurants, concert tickets, and a weekend stay at an exclusive resort. She checked their savings account and was furious to find the balance had dwindled again. Though she was sorely tempted to pick up the phone, Margo did not confront Chris herself. Instead, she called her attorney, Nancy, to let her know of the omission on Chris's financial disclosure. She simultaneously emailed Nancy with copies of the recent credit card charges and savings account statement.

Nancy asked Chris's attorney about these charges. Brian brushed them off. "My client is entitled to spend his own money and have a life," he said. "We'll true up at the end." Concerned at this response, Nancy immediately filed a motion with the court to enforce the financial moratorium on spending and requested that subpoenas be issued to all the known financial institutions. The judge, not wanting to waste the court's time, appointed a discovery master to take over the process of obtaining the necessary asset, debt, income, and spending information. Margo and Chris would meet, and pay for, a family law attorney who would ensure that all of the information was disclosed and each party held accountable for their lack of disclosure and transparency. Chris, who had been the most adamant about keeping lawyers to a minimum in their case, had managed, by deviating from the status quo and not being forthcoming in his financial statement, to add new legal complexity—and expense—to their divorce. Margo limited the financial fallout by being attentive to the financial activity in their accounts and going directly to her attorney with documentation of improper spending.

Regularly Monitor Your Financial Accounts

While your divorce is ongoing, it is critical that you pay routine attention to all your financial accounts. Closely review all activity and watch for any transactions that appear out of the ordinary. Your account balances and asset values will change, but you need to be able to discern typical fluctuations—those in keeping with your family's routine spending and your investment portfolios—from unusual changes in financial accounts that may signal illegitimate spending or the removal of funds.

To prepare your financial statement, you collected as much information as you could about your finances. If you haven't already, now is the time to obtain access to all your financial accounts: bank accounts, brokerage accounts, the mortgage, credit card statements, and tax returns. Now that your divorce is underway, your spouse may change passwords or financial institutions without your knowledge.

A spouse who cuts off your access to marital accounts is, at the very least, trying to take control of your shared finances and make your life more difficult. In some cases, they may also be trying to hide assets.

Spouses can get very creative in their attempts to conceal assets in a divorce. Some of the most common tactics include:

- Failing to inform you (through disclosure in their financial statement) about bank accounts, investments, property holdings, and other assets

- Withdrawing money from marital accounts and keeping it in cash

- Spending marital funds on valuables they intend to keep after the divorce

- Paying off "debts" to friends and family with the intent to recoup the money after the divorce

- Transferring cash, real estate, or investment holdings—stocks, bonds, commodities—to family or friends with the intent to reclaim the assets after the divorce

- Overpaying income taxes, expecting to receive the full refund after the divorce is final

- Delaying a bonus at work until after the divorce is final in order to keep the full value

It's important to understand that this improper behavior does happen, and to be watchful and attentive to your financial accounts throughout your divorce. It is also important to keep in mind that not every angry, controlling, vengeful spouse is hiding assets. To bring your hidden-asset claims to court, you will need proof. Your first step should be to take your documented concerns to your lawyer. The process of tracking down hidden assets is often difficult, expensive, and time-consuming. Before you decide to pursue a mission to track down hidden assets or expose your spouse's lying behavior, you need to evaluate whether it's worth it. You don't want to end up paying more in legal fees than the money you recoup. (I talk more about how to make these kinds of cost-benefit decisions in Chapter 7.) If you decide to proceed, depending on the amount at stake and the complexity of the financial circumstances, you may need to hire a forensic accountant to help you find and document your spouse's improper actions. Run the numbers to make sure it's worth the expense before you jump ahead.

Separate Your Credit from That of Your Spouse

Once your divorce is actively underway, it is time to remove your spouse's access to credit accounts in your name and close any joint credit card accounts you share. Ideally, you and your spouse will discuss this step as part of your plan to transition your financial lives to separate ones and decide together how to pay off balances and close joint accounts.

> ✔ **DO** take out a credit card in your own name, if you don't already have one, before you take any steps to close joint credit card accounts.

If there is a balance on your credit card account, you won't be able to close it, but you may be able to freeze the account from being used for new spending. You also may find you cannot close a joint credit card account without your spouse's authorization. If you and your spouse aren't cooperating with each other on this matter, work with the credit card company to freeze the account from accepting new charges. *Always put your requests to close or freeze joint accounts in writing and ask for written confirmation from the company that they have closed or frozen the account.* As always, if you and your spouse can work together in making these changes to your shared credit accounts, this process will be easier and move more quickly.

For as long as you and your spouse remain on joint cards, be sure to review your credit card statements carefully each month and stay alert for any unusual activity or inappropriate spending. If you find evidence of improper or excessive credit card spending, immediately take the preceding steps to cancel and/or cease your relationship with the credit accounts. Keep detailed records of the transactions and alert your lawyer and financial advisor.

> ✔ **DO** continue to pay at least the minimum balance on your credit cards to maintain your credit score.

Monitor Your Credit Reports

Your credit score will affect your financial future—for example, your ability to rent an apartment, obtain a mortgage, and get a car loan. While you're still financially connected to your spouse through debts and credit, their financial actions can impact your credit score. Your spouse may fail to pay bills on time or rack up debts by spending excessively. Sometimes spouses take out lines of credit in their spouse's name without their knowledge. If you're not already doing so, establish the habit of monitoring your credit reports every month to check your credit score. Be sure to review your credit activity and the list of debts that exist in your name.

There are three credit reporting agencies: TransUnion, Equifax, and Experian. Each has its own method of calculating credit scores, so don't be surprised when you see slightly different scores across different reports. Most credit card companies offer ongoing, real-time access to credit reports as well as credit monitoring services that alert you to unusual activity or changes in your credit report. You can also contact the credit reporting agencies directly to obtain copies of your credit reports, and you can access all three credit reports for free, once a year, at *www.annualcreditreport.com*.

Should We Close Our Joint Bank Accounts?

Many couples have at least one joint bank account that they've used for routine living expenses. During a divorce, spouses often opt to continue to use joint bank accounts to deposit their paychecks and pay their shared marital and household bills from the "operating budget."

However, if your spouse redirects their paycheck without informing you, then it is time to redirect your earnings to a bank account in your name. If you and your spouse are able to come to an agreement, you can decide to use the remaining funds for joint expenses during your divorce. If you're not able to reach an agreement about how you'll spend the remaining funds, you can split the balance and close the account.

Often, during divorce, a joint account is established for the sole purpose of managing the children's expenses. Each parent makes a regular, agreed-upon contribution, and the funds are used to pay for agreed-upon expenses—haircuts, school trips, sports fees, and the like—while the children are with each parent. This often requires a periodic true-up or audit in the event one parent has overspent, spent on unapproved items, or failed to make some of their monthly contributions.

Get Your Own Cell Phone Contract

If you and your spouse share a cell phone plan, your spouse has access to records of your phone calls and text messaging activity. They can track your movements and your locations. To keep your communications and your activity private and secure—and prevent your spouse from spying on you—you need your own cell phone contract.

I recommend getting one as early as possible, especially if you antici-pate your divorce will be contentious or if your spouse is controlling or vin-dictive. I've seen angry spouses use the family cell phone plan to control and punish their soon-to-be ex. One client of mine struggled for months to get his existing number released from a plan he shared with his spouse. As is often the case, keeping his number was important to him. It was the number his children's schools, coaches, and doctors all had, not to mention all his professional and personal contacts going back several years. The account was held in his spouse's name and my client needed his spouse to give the cell phone company permission to release the telephone number for transfer to another carrier. To my client's deep frustration and anger, his spouse refused. It was a maddening episode for my client, taking up many hours of his time and much of his valuable emotional energy.

> ✔ **DO** be sure your name is on the account, if you decide to remain on a shared plan during your divorce. This gives you access and control over the plan if you need to make a change.

Pay Careful Attention to Your Taxes

You will likely need to file taxes while your divorce is in process. The financial limbo of not-yet-divorced can be especially tricky at tax time. You need to decide how you will file. And if you file jointly with your spouse, you need to review your taxes very carefully for accuracy in your spouse's reporting. You have two options for filing during a divorce:

MARRIED FILING JOINTLY

You and your spouse file one return, reporting all your earned income, withholdings, deductions, and credits. For many still-married filers, this may provide you with greater tax benefits than filing separately.

There is risk in filing jointly with your spouse, because when you do so you are legally responsible for the information on that return and any tax liability or penalty that arises from your spouse's taxable transactions, even if you weren't aware of the activity or didn't receive any of the proceeds. Under these circumstances you can ask the court for relief from responsibility for paying the taxes, interest, and penalties owed by invoking what's known as the "Innocent Spouse Rule." By doing so, you are claiming you should not be held responsible for the tax liability, because you were unaware of what was reported in the tax return and signed it at the direction of (or pressure from) your spouse. This defense can work, but it can be expensive, time-consuming, and stressful, and you may not prevail.

If you are filing joint income tax returns, be sure to review them carefully yourself or better yet, have your own accountant (not your spouse's) review them to ensure that all information is accurate.

MARRIED FILING SEPARATELY

You and your spouse each file separate tax returns with your own income, withholdings, deductions, and credits. If you have concerns about your spouse's reporting during your divorce, this may be the better option for you. This also may be a good choice if you have a low income, as you may be eligible for additional tax benefits. If you are a high earner, this option may cost you more in taxes.

I recommend adding a CPA to your team to advise you on how best to file during your divorce and assist you in preparing your tax returns during this transitional time in your financial life. This professional can also work with you and your financial advisor to assess the tax implications of settlement proposals you create or receive from your spouse.

> ✔ **DO** anticipate a change in filing during the calendar year your divorce is resolved. You can file jointly (or married filing separately) while your divorce is in progress. During the tax year when your divorce is final, you must file as single or head of household for that year. Your tax status for filing purposes is determined by your marital status on December 31.

Review Your Health Insurance

To ensure that your family maintains continuous health insurance coverage during your divorce, familiarize yourself with the details of your existing insurance policies. You need to understand how your state's laws, and the employers and insurance policy involved, address divorce as an event that changes coverage. You have options to consider, and now is the time to start planning and budgeting what best suits your changing family's health insurance needs and financial circumstances.

If you and your spouse are each covered under your own policies, whether purchased individually or accessed through your employer, then your health insurance won't need to change as a result of your divorce. If you have children, you and your spouse will need to come to an agreement about how you will provide for their health insurance after you're divorced. If your children are covered under your spouse's employer-based health care plan (or yours), they can remain on that policy. It's important that your final divorce agreement make clear provisions for how you and your spouse will contribute to the health care costs not covered by insurance. (I talk more about children's health insurance and medical costs as a component of your settlement in Chapter 6.)

If you are covered under your spouse's employer-based group health insurance plan, check to see if you are eligible to remain on the plan post-divorce. Some companies will allow a former spouse to take out their own policy on the group plan, often with a higher premium. You can negotiate to have the premium paid by your ex as part of your support package, or you can take on the payments yourself if this option fits your budget. If you cannot remain on your current group plan after your divorce, you have other options:

JOIN A GROUP POLICY THROUGH YOUR EMPLOYER. If you're currently working outside the home and your employer offers health insurance benefits, consider taking advantage of this benefit. This is also an option to keep in mind for the longer term if you're not currently employed but anticipate getting a job during or after your divorce.

ACQUIRE TEMPORARY COVERAGE THROUGH COBRA. The Consolidated Omnibus Budget Reconciliation Act, or COBRA, is a federal law that allows you to stay on your ex-spouse's employer-based group health insurance for up to thirty-six months after your coverage through your spouse ends. You can negotiate for your spouse to cover the monthly COBRA payment for some or all of the coverage period. If your spouse isn't covering this as part of your agreement, you will be responsible for the premiums. COBRA mandates that you cannot be charged more than the monthly premium for other participants in the group plan who are receiving the same benefits. (There is a 2 percent administrative charge that is added to COBRA premiums.) COBRA is a temporary solution; your coverage will last no longer than thirty-six months and will end sooner if you remarry. COBRA is expensive, but it can be a good bridge until you find less expensive coverage.

OBTAIN CONTINUATION COVERAGE THROUGH YOUR STATE. Some states have laws similar to the federal COBRA law that provide divorcing spouses the option to continue participating in group health insurance coverage that they received through their spouse. Some states offer a longer coverage duration and lower costs than COBRA. Ask your attorney and your financial advisor about health care continuation coverage offered by your state.

PURCHASE COVERAGE THROUGH THE ACA. You can buy health insurance through the Affordable Care Act health insurance marketplace. Purchasing individual health insurance can be expensive, but the ACA provides financial subsidies depending on your income. Go to *www.healthcare.gov* to find out about ACA insurance options in your state.

SIGN UP FOR MEDICAID. If you don't have income or if your income is limited, you can apply for Medicaid. Medicaid coverage is available through your state. Contact your local Medicaid office to find out about income requirements and how to apply.

SIGN UP FOR MEDICARE. At age sixty-five, you can enroll in Medicare. If you are disabled, you may be able to enroll sooner. You are eligible for Medicare whether or not you have paid Medicare taxes through employment. You also can purchase supplemental Medicare, known as Medigap insurance, to cover Medicare deductibles, copayments, and coinsurance. You can learn more about Medicare at *www.medicare.gov*. And AARP (*www.aarp.org*) is a valuable resource for information about Medicare and other retirement-related topics.

🔥 *Red Flag* During your divorce, you can't change beneficiaries on life insurance policies, retirement accounts, or other financial accounts. But you can change nonfinancial documents to update trusted contacts and assign people to act on your behalf if you die or are unable to temporarily manage your affairs while your divorce is in progress. If you have appointed your spouse as your health care proxy (also known as medical power of attorney), consider contacting your lawyer to change that now. You may not want your soon-to-be ex deciding whether you live or die. If you don't have a health care proxy, establish one now to ensure that your spouse is not involved in making medical decisions on your behalf while you're going through a divorce. In addition to updating your health care proxy, update—or create—your power of attorney and living will directives so that you're confident your wishes will be enacted during the limbo period of your divorce if the worst happens. (I talk more about these important estate-planning documents in Chapter 9.)

★ *Gabrielle's Pro Tip*   Health savings accounts (HSA) frequently get overlooked in divorce agreements. If you or your spouse has an HSA that you contributed to during your marriage, this may be considered a marital asset. HSAs, which are available with some high-deductible insurance plans, allow you to save pretax dollars to put toward paying health care costs, including deductibles, copayments and coinsurance, prescriptions, and medical expenses. Your family's HSA may have a significant balance. As part of your divorce agreement, you and your spouse may be able to agree to use the HSA funds accrued during your marriage to cover family medical expenses that aren't fully covered by insurance.

Track Your Spending

One of the biggest mistakes people make during a divorce is failing to be realistic about their spending. If you cannot accurately and comprehensively account for your expenses, you are likely to receive a reduced level of support in your final settlement. Using the information you compiled for your financial statement and the budget worksheets later in this chapter, make a detailed inventory of your expenses. Review your credit cards, checking accounts, mobile payment apps (Venmo, PayPal), and automatic bill pay services to accurately document all your spending. Know your numbers and track every penny you spend, so you can make informed decisions when it's time to consider a financial settlement. The proposed support in a settlement offer may seem like enough money. But when you compare it against your expenses, you may be surprised.

You may not like the financial picture your budget shows you. Your new financial reality may require you to cut back spending, downsize

your home, and/or get a job. But understanding the reality of your financial circumstances is how you begin to take control of your finances *now*
to avoid financial crisis *later.*

★ *Gabrielle's Pro Tip* If you are working with a divorce financial advisor,
they can do an analysis of your cash flow to help you understand your family's
spending habits. A cash flow analysis can be an important tool for establishing
your marital standard of living, which may be a factor in determining support
amounts and dividing your marital property. A cash flow analysis is of strategic
help when you are considering how to divide your assets and whether to sell a
home, stocks, collectibles, or other property as part of your divorce settlement.
It will also be a significant help to you in building a budget for the transitional
period of divorce and for your post-divorce life.

Track Your Children's Expenses Separately

To determine child support, you will be expected to substantiate your
children's financial needs. You will need to accurately document their
current expenses—and you need to be proactive by anticipating and
projecting future ones. Therapy, driver's education, tutoring, medical
copays, afterschool childcare, fees for sports or lessons, clothing and
sports uniforms—now is the time to get a handle on the costs of raising
your children. Get organized. Designate one of your credit cards exclusively for your children's expenses or highlight and color-code child-related expenses on your current credit card statements. Use Quicken or
build an Excel spreadsheet and record every child-related expense you
incur. Establish a routine for updating the spreadsheet or online record
every week. Keep your paper receipts and ask for email or electronic
receipts. Copy the receipts and upload them to a Dropbox folder or online
file cabinet.

To help your family succeed in the financial transition of divorce, you
must understand—and be able to show the court—how much it will cost
to raise your children.

★ *Gabrielle's Pro Tip*   There are several apps that help coparents track and manage children's expenses. See the resources section at the end of this book for a list of apps you and your spouse can use.

Work Through Your Options for Your Marital Home

For reasons financial, emotional, and logistical, figuring out how to handle your marital home is often one of the most difficult decisions in a divorce. Your home may be your most valuable financial asset. Your home is also the place where you've made family memories and established relationships in a community. Now is the time to evaluate what options are possible—and desirable—for you and your family.

DO YOU WANT TO STAY IN YOUR HOME?

Many people don't want the home because it carries too many emotional memories, good and bad. Consider the benefits and drawbacks of your location in the context of your future life. A client of mine, Clare, has four young children and decided she didn't want to keep her large home because it felt like too much to manage. She wanted to be closer to the schools her children would attend in a few years, and within walking distance to town and the park. That said, if your neighborhood offers an important support system for you and your children, if you can afford it you may want to consider staying put until the kids get older and downsize then.

Ask yourself: *Will I be happier making a fresh start in a new home? What are the advantages and disadvantages for my family in staying in the home and neighborhood, or moving to a new house and neighborhood?*

CAN YOU AFFORD YOUR HOME?

Once you've completed your financial statement and have a sense of how much support you will be receiving or paying, you will have an understanding of how much of your budget your home will require. The mortgage, home maintenance, homeowner's insurance, and real estate taxes are all typically higher in a larger home. *Fixed housing costs—mortgage or rent, insurance, and property taxes—should not exceed 25 percent of your net income.* If you don't have the cash flow to support the house and pay the bills, then keeping the house will hurt you more than it helps you. If you fall behind on your mortgage or car payment, your credit score will suffer, which will have a negative impact on your ability to refinance or qualify for credit in the future. Keeping up with a house that you can't afford is stressful. If you can't maintain the home and it falls into disrepair, the value will go down, and larger repair and maintenance problems could develop, which, if left unaddressed, will drive up your costs further.

Selling and downsizing can also free up cash to help you pay down debts at the time of your divorce, rather than carry marital debt obligations into your new, post-divorce future.

Ask yourself: *Will keeping the house cause me to be house poor—low on cash and high on house? Is that how I want to spend the next chapter of my life? Are there other financial priorities I can address by selling and downsizing?*

✔ **DO** consider getting your own appraiser before you begin negotiating in order to get a good idea of the true value of your home. If you and your spouse agree that one of you will buy the other out, you will need to have another appraisal done. But an early appraisal can help you prepare for negotiations and help you think your way through your decisions about the house.

Creating a Budget for Your Changing Family

Now that your divorce is underway, it's time to establish a budget that will guide your spending and your financial decision-making throughout your divorce and beyond. You compiled the raw material for your budget when you documented your income and expenses to get a handle on your cash flow. But there are some important differences. Your cash flow was a snapshot of your recent earning and spending during your marriage. Your budget will be a projection of your income and expenses in your new household, and a financial blueprint for the adjustments you intend to make to your spending and earning as you undergo the financial changes of your divorce.

Your budget is always a dynamic document—and that's especially true during a divorce. You can expect your budget to change as you make decisions and adjustments associated with your divorce, which may include working out a parenting schedule, moving and downsizing your home, getting a job, and reducing your expenses to bring them in line with your changing household income. Your budget will be a work in progress that will:

- Help you understand your family's changing cash flow as you transition to two households

- Guide you to adjust your spending to bring your expenses in line with your income

- Document your need for child and/or spousal support, based on your income and your children's financial needs

- Document your capacity and responsibility to provide child and/or spousal support, based on your income and your children's financial needs

- Provide you with a detailed, forward-looking financial picture you can use to develop financial settlement proposals and evaluate settlement offers from your spouse

BUDGET WORKSHEETS

There are two components to creating a budget: your income and your expenses. You can account for income and expenses weekly, monthly, or annually. Most people prefer a monthly budget since they are paid once or twice a month and most expenses occur monthly, but it doesn't matter—what matters is that you have one and that you use it to guide and inform your everyday financial decisions and your financial planning for the future. This is your budget. Set it up in the way that works best for you. The following worksheets guide you through categorizing and tallying your income and expenses on a monthly basis.

★ *Gabrielle's Pro Tip* If you're using a weekly, biweekly, or monthly budget, you need to accurately account for income and expenses that occur annually or irregularly. The best way to do that is to look at your most recent year of income and expenditures and get an annual total for each of the income sources and expenses that occur annually, seasonally, or otherwise irregularly. Divide each annual total by twelve to get a figure that represents your monthly earnings or costs, and add each one to your income or expense worksheets.

Budgeting Your Net Monthly Income

Include your gross income for your monthly earnings and any other income sources.

If you anticipate receiving child support and/or spousal support, use your state's online calculator to get an estimate of the support you may receive, based on your income and your spouse's income. If you are receiving support through temporary orders from the court, you can use those amounts here. *In either scenario, it's essential to keep in mind that these estimated and temporary support amounts are not guaranteed until your divorce is final.*

Using your pay stubs from the most recent month, add the monthly total of your deductions for federal, state, and local taxes; insurance premiums; FICA (Social Security and Medicare); pretax contributions to retirement plans and/or health savings accounts; and any other deductions.

Subtract your total monthly deductions from your total gross income to identify your net monthly income. This is the monthly influx of funds you have to pay your bills and support your household.

INCOME	MONTHLY INCOME	NOTES
Gross income from employment wages		
Gross income from self-employment		
Social Security		
Disability		
Worker's compensation		
Retirement income:		
Retirement accounts (401(k), 403(b), IRAs)		
Pension		
Annuity		
Other		
Dividend income		
Interest income		
Trust income		
Royalties		

INCOME	MONTHLY INCOME	NOTES
Rental property		
Child support from previous marriage		
Spousal support from previous marriage		
Interim or anticipated spousal support*		
Interim or anticipated child support*		
Total gross monthly income:		

*Whether you are receiving interim support or estimating support amounts using your state's calculators and formulas, keep in mind that these dollar figures are not guaranteed to be what you will receive when your divorce is final. Use interim or estimated support figures to help yourself plan, and stay prepared for the reality that these figures may change in your final settlement.

DEDUCTIONS	MONTHLY DEDUCTION	NOTES
Taxes:		
Federal		
State		
Local		
FICA (Social Security and Medicare)		

DEDUCTIONS	MONTHLY DEDUCTION	NOTES
Self-employment taxes (income, FICA)		
Pretax insurance premiums: medical, dental, vision, life, disability		
Health savings account contribution		
Retirement and employer-benefit contributions: 401(k), pension, etc.		
Total monthly deductions:		

Total gross monthly income:	
Total monthly deductions:	
Monthly net income:	

Budgeting Your Expenses

Below are basic templates for expenses in major categories, including home, living, child, vehicle, entertainment and travel, and health care expenses. Customize your list of expenses in each category to accurately reflect all your monthly bills and obligations.

Add the total expenses for each category to arrive at a cumulative total of your monthly expenses.

If you anticipate paying child support and/or spousal support, use your state's online calculator to get an estimate of the support you may need to pay, based on your income and your spouse's income. Include anticipated support payments in the cumulative total of your monthly expenses. If you are paying support through temporary orders from the court, you can use those amounts here. In either scenario, it's essential to keep in mind that these interim and estimated support figures are not guaranteed to be the support you will be obligated to pay when your divorce is final.

HOME EXPENSES	MONTHLY EXPENSE	NOTES
Mortgage or rent		
Home equity loan		
Association fees		
Property taxes		
Homeowner's insurance		
Renter's insurance		
Electric		
Heat (gas, oil, etc.)		
Water		

HOME EXPENSES	MONTHLY EXPENSE	NOTES
Sewer		
Internet		
Cable/satellite TV		
Telephone (landline)		
Housecleaning services		
Lawn/garden services		
Snowplow services		
Pool services		
Routine maintenance		
Major repair and maintenance		
Other		
Other		
Total monthly home expenses:		

LIVING EXPENSES	MONTHLY EXPENSE	NOTES
Groceries		
Liquor		
Household supplies		
Dry cleaning/laundry services		
Clothing (yours)		
Personal care supplies		
Personal care services		
Pet care (food, supplies, medical care, insurance)		
Memberships and club dues		
Adult education		
Gifts		
Charitable donations		
Cash for miscellaneous		
Other		
Other		
Total monthly living expenses:		

CHILDREN	MONTHLY EXPENSE	NOTES
Clothing		
Childcare at home		
Daycare		
Tuition		
Afterschool childcare		
Tutoring		
Program and activity fees		
School/program/activity supplies and equipment		
Transportation		
Cash for miscellaneous		
Other		
Other		
Total monthly children's expenses:		

ENTERTAINMENT, RECREATION, AND TRAVEL	MONTHLY EXPENSE	NOTES
Dining out		
Catering/entertaining		
Events (movies, concerts, sporting events)		
Streaming services (video, music)		
Books, magazine/newspaper subscriptions		
Travel (transportation, lodging, dining, recreation)		
Hobbies		
Other		
Other		
Total monthly entertainment expenses:		

VEHICLE EXPENSES	MONTHLY EXPENSE	NOTES
Loan		
Lease		
Fuel		
Maintenance and repair		
Parking/tolls		
Storage		
Other		
Other		
Total monthly vehicle expenses:		

NON-EMPLOYER-BASED INSURANCE PREMIUMS	MONTHLY EXPENSE	NOTES
Medical		
Dental		
Vision		
Prescription		
Life		
Long-term care		
Disability		
Personal liability		
Other		
Total monthly non-employer-based insurance premium expenses:		

HEALTH CARE COSTS NOT COVERED BY INSURANCE	YOU	YOUR CHILDREN	NOTES
Medical			
Dental			
Vision			
Prescription			
Mental health			
Wellness services (massage, nutrition, etc.)			
Other			
Other			
Total monthly health care costs not covered by insurance			

MONTHLY EXPENSES TALLY	MONTHLY AMOUNT	NOTES
Home		
Living		
Children		
Entertainment, recreation, travel		
Vehicles		
Insurance		
Health care costs not covered by insurance (you and your children)		
Interim or anticipated support payments (child and/or spousal support)*		
Total monthly expenses:		

* Whether you are receiving interim support or estimating support amounts using your state's calculators and formulas, keep in mind that these dollar figures are not guaranteed to be what you will receive when your divorce is final. Use interim or estimated support figures to help yourself plan, and stay prepared for the reality that these figures may change in your final settlement.

Your Budgeted Cash Flow

To see your monthly cash flow, subtract your total monthly income from your total monthly expenses. This will tell you whether your budgeted income will cover your expenses or you will be spending more than you earn.

Total monthly net income:	
Total expenses:	
Monthly cash flow:	

Dos and Don'ts for Budgeting During Your Divorce

✔ **DO** track your income and expenses consistently and adjust your budget periodically to reflect your most up-to-date earning and spending.

✔ **DO** use Quicken or another online financial management program to create and maintain your household budget. These programs make it easy to build a budget and update it regularly, so that it remains an accurate and useful financial resource for you during your divorce and after.

✔ **DO** make sure that your net income is equal to or exceeds your expenses. Otherwise, how are you covering your bills? *This is where you can run into financial trouble: depleting savings, running up credit card debt, and needing to borrow against your assets to stay afloat.*

✔ **DO** use your state's online support calculators to determine the amount of child support and/or spousal support you are likely to receive, based on your income and your spouse's income. Include those estimates in the income section of your budget. *But remember, these amounts are not guaranteed until your divorce is final.*

✖ **DON'T** forget that support can be modified over time, as your income or your ex-spouse's income changes.

✔ **DO** keep records of your expenses during (and after) your divorce. You may need to defend your expenses with documentation in negotiation or in court.

✔ **DO** keep records of your big expenditures and be prepared to defend them in the event your spouse accuses you of dissipating marital assets.

✖ **DON'T** inflate your expenses to attempt to get more support. Your spouse likely has a sense of what you need to live. The numbers tell a story—and you may need to defend that story with documentation in court.

✖ **DON'T** underestimate your expenses. Be honest, detailed, and thorough.

✔ **DO** be consistent with your data entry. Your numbers won't tell an accurate story of your cash flow and spending patterns if they aren't complete and up to date.

✔ **DO** make it fun! You'll feel empowered to know that you can pay your bills with the income you have.

Key Takeaways and Next Steps

- During your divorce, pay careful attention to your finances. Keep your spending in line with how you spent money during your marriage, track and record your expenses carefully, and regularly monitor your financial accounts.

- You're still connected financially to your spouse while your divorce is ongoing, but you can take steps to establish your independent financial life. Close (or freeze) joint credit cards and open a credit card in your own name if you don't already have one. Routinely monitor your credit report and watch out for any new debts in your name that you are unfamiliar with. Get your own cell phone contract.

- Talk with a CPA about how best to file your taxes during your divorce.

- Anticipate—and budget for—upcoming changes in health insurance coverage for you and/or your children.

- Create a new household budget and work to reduce expenses and live within your means as your income changes.

CHAPTER SIX

From Ours to Mine and Yours

The Building Blocks of a Financial Settlement

Financial negotiation in divorce is about determining the best, most equitable and sustainable way to divide your marital estate and apportion support. This is where you work to craft the business deal that ends your married, *interdependent* financial life and begins your *independent* financial life.

Depending on the process you have chosen to resolve your case, you may be negotiating directly with your spouse. If you're using mediation, you will have a mediator to guide you through those discussions, and you should be consulting regularly with your attorney and your financial advisor to ensure you have the information you need to make sound, appropriate decisions in mediation sessions. If you're using the collaborative process, you and your spouse will be working out the terms of your divorce with your lawyers and other professionals supporting and advising you as a unified team. If you're litigating your divorce, your lawyer is negotiating for you, with your input. Regardless of the method you're using, you are not a bystander to this process. You are a critical participant in your divorce negotiations. Remember, at the end of the day, the lawyers go home, and you are left with an agreement that governs your future.

You've done the legwork to be a smart, informed participant in your negotiations. You've developed a firm grasp of your financial circumstances and the full spectrum of income, assets, and debts at stake in your divorce. You've spent time formulating a vision for the next chapter of your life—the hopes, dreams, and goals you want your financial settlement to help you achieve. You've created a budget that tells you what your expenses are and what income you need to support your household. You've worked on a plan to bridge the gap between your income and your expenses by earning more, spending less, and being thoughtful and efficient in how you use your money.

Negotiating your financial settlement is where the jigsaw puzzle comes together, and there are many moving pieces to consider. The laws of your state set forth the guidelines and formulas for you to follow. Within that legal framework, however, there's a lot that can go right, and wrong. Throughout your negotiations, you will work with your attorney and financial advisor to develop a settlement proposal that meets your needs and priorities, and to evaluate proposals and counteroffers from your spouse. To do that you need to think rationally, realistically, and strategically about all the components of your agreement.

Divorce negotiations understandably can make you feel nervous and under pressure. This is a process that takes time. Sometimes it will feel like a marathon, and other times like a sprint. There will be periods of relative quiet, punctuated by flurries of activity and decision-making. While your negotiations are in progress, take care of yourself. Rest as much as you can. Lean on your emotional support team. Fill your cup with things that make you feel good physically, emotionally, and spiritually. On any given day, that might be exercise, or an afternoon on the couch with a book or a movie. It might be daily meditation or prayer. It may be time with your children, time to yourself, time with dear friends. Find your peace and your solace where it resides for you. And ask for help and support often.

We're going to cover a lot of important ground in this chapter. As you move through negotiating the components of your financial settlement, you can return to this chapter to refresh your memory and home in on the specifics of the negotiation issues that are top of mind at every step.

Determining Child Support

A quick review of the basics: Child support is calculated according to state law using its child support guidelines. The calculations consider your income, your spouse's income, and the amount of time the children will be in the care of each parent. Depending on state guidelines, calculated child support amounts are often reduced to account for the paying spouse's financial contributions to the children's medical insurance, dental insurance, and childcare expenses. (See the next section for more detail on planning for children's medical expenses in your divorce agreement.)

Child support is intended to cover the basic, essential costs of caring for children, including food, clothing, and shelter. Each state has its own guidelines that define which expenses child support provides for, and some states set much broader definitions of the essentials than others. Regardless of how broad and inclusive the child support guidelines are in your state, there are always costs that go beyond the basics. **Beyond child support, your agreement should include a comprehensive, forward-looking plan for all the costs child support won't cover.** Your settlement agreement needs to include a provision that lays out specifically all the expenses associated with your children that aren't considered in child support calculations, and how each parent will contribute financially to these costs. If you've thoroughly documented all your children's current expenses and you understand what expenses child support is expected to address according to your state's guidelines, then you can identify in detail the additional expenses that you need a plan to cover. Make sure your settlement addresses precisely how you and your spouse will share in each of these current expenses. Your provision may also include plans to share equitably in some future expenses you anticipate for your children, based on your children's needs and the lifestyle your children have led during your marriage. When future expenses for children are planned for in a divorce agreement, they are generally either highly anticipated expenses (such as driver's education or SAT prep courses) or expenses that are in keeping with the children's lifestyle during your marriage (such as sleepaway camp, or the evolving costs of sports and other activities your children currently participate in). As part of a provision to share in expenses beyond the basics covered by child support, divorcing parents often set a dollar figure that limits joint child expenses without upfront agreement. For example, you and your spouse might decide that any child-related expense over $250 or $500 that is to be shared between you must be agreed to by you both.

> ✔ **DO** put your plan in writing, in detail, as part of your final agreement even when you anticipate working amicably and cooperatively with your soon-to-be ex-spouse to share in the financial costs of raising your children.

Some families opt to maintain a joint checking account and make monthly contributions to cover child-related expenses they have agreed to share: birthday presents for friends, special occasions, Mother/Father's Day gifts, holiday gifts, tutors, driving lessons, and the like.

★ *Gabrielle's Pro Tip*   You and your spouse know your family best. There are no two people better equipped to identify and anticipate your children's current and future needs. If possible, work together to come up with a cost-sharing plan that embodies your family values for supporting and enriching the lives of your children.

ARRANGING HEALTH INSURANCE AS PART OF YOUR CHILD SUPPORT AGREEMENT

During negotiations, you and your spouse will need to work out arrangements for your children's health insurance coverage and uninsured medical and dental expenses. Federal law mandates that your child support agreement address how you and your spouse will provide health care coverage for your children. If your children are covered under one spouse's employer-based health insurance coverage, you and your spouse may decide to continue with that arrangement, or you may agree to buy a new insurance plan for your children. Depending on your family's financial circumstances and how your state calculates child support amounts, a spouse who is paying the cost of health care insurance for children may pay less child support or receive additional support to compensate.

If you cannot agree to a plan for paying for your children's health insurance and medical costs, as with all components of your settlement, the court will decide for you. In some cases, a spouse with employer-based coverage (or their insurance company or employer) may refuse to keep or add their children on their health insurance plan. Under those circumstances, the other parent can get a court order that allows them to obtain health care benefits for their children through their spouse's employer-based coverage. The Qualified Medical Child Support Order (QMSCO) can also order that the premiums be paid from the insurance-holding spouse's paycheck, and that the insurance-holding spouse choose a plan that provides sufficient coverage for their children.

Your agreement should also include a detailed plan for how you and your spouse will share in the expenses for your children's health care that aren't covered by insurance, including the costs of meeting annual insurance deductibles and copayments; vision, hearing, and dental care (including orthodontia) that isn't covered by insurance; and any other medical care or therapy costs you don't expect insurance to cover. If you don't articulate precisely how you and your ex will share in these expenses after you're divorced, you may find yourself down the road having to shoulder a larger portion of these costs than you can afford, or returning to court to request an increase in support or a contribution from your ex.

> ✔ **DO** contact your state's Medicaid office if you and your spouse have limited income and can't afford insurance. State-run Medicaid programs provide medical, dental, and vision insurance for children in households with limited income.

FUNDING COLLEGE IN A DIVORCE AGREEMENT

College expenses are not considered in child support calculations. Although it is in the child's best interest, state laws do not require parents to pay for children's college educations. (That said, depending on the circumstances of your case, including parents' incomes and assets and the ages of your children, a judge may want to see college expenses addressed in your divorce agreement.) You can include a provision in your agreement that addresses how you and your spouse will contribute to your children's college expenses. If you do, be clear about which expenses you and your spouse will cover and how much each of you will contribute. Depending on your circumstances, you may decide to:

SPLIT 50-50 THE COLLEGE COSTS YOU'VE AGREED TO FUND. If you and your spouse have similar incomes and assets after your divorce, this may be an option to consider.

SPLIT AGREED-UPON COSTS PROPORTIONALLY, IN LINE WITH YOUR INCOMES. This may make sense if one spouse has significantly higher earnings than the other. You may consider splitting all expenses proportionally or agreeing to have the higher-earning spouse pay tuition and room and board, while the lower-earning spouse agrees to pay for books, supplies, and incidental expenses.

AGREE TO CONTRIBUTE TO COLLEGE EDUCATION SAVINGS ACCOUNTS SUCH AS 529S OR OTHER TAX-EXEMPT OR TAX-DEFERRED ACCOUNTS. You and your spouse may agree to periodic payments, or you may consider using a portion of the assets you're dividing in your divorce to fund education savings accounts or educational trusts in a lump sum.

DECIDE NOT TO INCLUDE A COLLEGE FUNDING PLAN AS PART OF YOUR DIVORCE AGREEMENT. Some spouses opt not to include specific plans for funding college at the time of their divorce. You and your spouse may choose to work out those arrangements when your children near college age. You may decide you cannot afford or don't want to commit to paying college costs. Be realistic about your current and projected financial capabilities at the time of your divorce. It may make sense for your family to revisit the college funding question down the road, when you can include your children in the conversation and explore options for loans, scholarships, financial aid, work study, and part-time jobs.

SUPPORTING A CHILD WITH SPECIAL NEEDS

Make sure the language in your agreement is clear in identifying all the expenses associated with minor children who have special needs, and how you and your spouse will each contribute to paying those expenses. Divorce agreements typically do not provide for or mandate support for a child who has reached the age of emancipation, because it is not enforceable in a court of law. (To be effective, an agreement must be enforceable.) Each state has rules and guidelines for the age and circumstances at which child support ends.

There are federal benefits that help support people with special needs as they become adults, including Social Security Supplemental Income and Social Security Disability Insurance (SSDI). *Special needs trusts* are designed to help support a child without jeopardizing that child's eligibility to receive state and federal benefits.

An ABLE (Achieving a Better Life Experience) account, also known as a 529 ABLE, is a state-based, tax-advantaged savings program (similar to a 529) designed to provide financial support to help pay for qualified disability expenses of a beneficiary/owner.

During your divorce, consult a special-needs attorney for advice about establishing a provision in your agreement that articulates a plan for you and your ex-spouse to provide for your child with special needs during their years as a minor and as they grow into adulthood.

Determining Spousal Support

Spousal support calculations are based on income. Spousal support is sometimes, but not always, determined after child support has been calculated. Eligibility to receive alimony is based on the recipient's need and the paying spouse's ability to pay. Alimony is not taxable to the recipient, nor is it tax-deductible for the paying spouse. The duration of spousal support depends on the guidelines of the state where your case resides. The most common factors affecting the duration of spousal support are the length of the marriage; the marital lifestyle; the recipient's age, health, and ability to work; and the disparity between the recipient's and paying spouse's incomes.

A LUMP SUM VS. PERIODIC PAYMENTS FOR ALIMONY

Alimony can be paid periodically, typically on a monthly basis. Often, however, divorcing spouses consider using a lump-sum payment for spousal support—often referred to as an *alimony buyout*. One lump sum is paid to the recipient and the paying spouse has no further obligation to provide support.

Arriving at the right lump-sum value can be more of an art than a science. It's generally done by first determining *net present value*—a calculation of the *current value* of the total, agreed-upon sum of money that would be paid periodically over an agreed-upon number of months or years. Net present value is found by calculating the total amount of support (the amount of the monthly payment multiplied by the total number of months that support would be paid over time) and then applying a discount rate. Why is a discount rate applied? In a nutshell, because funds in possession now are more valuable to the recipient than the promise of funds to be paid in the future.

> ✖ **DON'T** assume your attorney can undertake financial calculations on your behalf. Consult your financial advisor or CPA if you are negotiating a lump-sum amount for spousal support.

In many cases, the biggest obstacle in employing a lump-sum buyout is funding. For a buyout to be possible, the paying spouse must have the money to fund the lump-sum payment. They may use a portion of the marital assets, take out a loan and borrow the funds, or pay in cash with outside or separate assets (perhaps an advance on an inheritance or other future financial expectation). In some cases, the paying spouse will pay the lump sum in installments over a short number of months, rather than all at once. If fully funding a lump-sum payment isn't possible, you and your spouse can also consider a partial lump-sum arrangement, where the paying spouse pays a lump sum that covers a portion of the total alimony and pays monthly support in smaller amounts and/or for a shorter period of time.

There are clear upsides to the lump-sum route for both the paying spouse and the recipient. The recipient receives their support while facing none of the uncertainties that come with periodic payments: *Will your spouse stop paying? Will they lose their job or experience a change in income that could reduce payments? Do you have the insurance to protect spousal support if your ex dies or becomes disabled and unable to work?* The paying spouse completes their support obligation right up front and avoids having to pay their ex for months and years to come. There are other factors to consider for both spouses before deciding to structure spousal support in a lump sum.

A recipient of spousal support should pursue a lump-sum payment if:

YOU ARE CONCERNED THAT YOUR EX WILL FAIL TO PAY. If your former spouse doesn't meet their obligations to make periodic payments, you will have to go to court to force them to pay. Chasing down spousal support is stressful and time-consuming, and you will have to pay legal fees.

YOU ARE CONCERNED THAT YOUR EX WILL LOSE THEIR JOB. If your former spouse loses their income, they can return to court to request a modification based on a change of circumstances, and you could lose your support permanently, or at least until they get a new job.

YOU DON'T WANT TO BE TETHERED TO YOUR EX FOR THE DURATION OF THE ALIMONY TERM. Paying spousal support is not something that ex-spouses typically like to do. Extending spousal support over a period of months or years can cause animosity in your post-divorce relationship, which can be especially difficult if you have children together.

YOU DON'T WANT TO BE BOUND BY THE LEGAL RESTRICTIONS ASSOCIATED WITH ALIMONY IN YOUR STATE. Many states will allow your ex to terminate alimony if you remarry, live with a romantic partner, or earn over a certain amount of money (because you no longer "need" the money; you can support yourself).

YOU HAVE CONCERNS ABOUT YOUR EX'S HEALTH. You need to consider the likelihood that your spouse will not meet the full financial obligation due to death or disability. If your spouse is in poor health and does not have life insurance, a lump-sum payment is a good option for you.

A spouse paying spousal support should pursue a lump-sum payment if:

YOU EXPECT TO EARN MORE MONEY IN THE FUTURE. Your former spouse may be able to take you back to court for an increase in spousal support if your income changes. If you are earning a lot more than you were when the spousal support order was calculated, you may face a higher obligation.

YOU WANT TO BE FREE TO MOVE ON. Paying monthly alimony will keep you fiscally involved with your ex, which may have a negative effect on your post-divorce relationship or require you to have a relationship when you wouldn't otherwise have or want one.

YOU DON'T WANT ANOTHER MONTHLY OBLIGATION BURDENING YOUR CASH FLOW. If you can fund a lump-sum payment from your share of the assets, it will free up your monthly cash flow as you begin your post-divorce life.

A paying spouse should avoid a lump-sum payment if:

YOUR EMPLOYMENT IS IN JEOPARDY. If you are terminated, you may petition the court to lower or end altogether your spousal support payments. If you voluntarily quit your job, however, your support may not be terminated and you may have to honor the obligation by dipping into your savings or retirement or taking a job below your qualifications.

YOU ARE CONCERNED THAT YOUR EX WILL MISMANAGE THE MONEY AND ATTEMPT TO COME BACK FOR MORE. Consider your spouse's experience with managing money. If there are substance abuse issues or demonstrated concerns around money, periodic payments may be best, as they may protect your ex's ability to support themselves.

Protecting Child and Spousal Support with Life Insurance

Life insurance is a core component of child and spousal support agreements. If you are receiving support payments for yourself and/or your children, it is critical that you have life insurance in place to ensure you receive the support you're entitled to in the event your former spouse dies before their support obligations have been met.

Make sure the insurance is in place *before* you sign the agreement. Agreements often state that the paying spouse "will apply" for insurance after the divorce, only for the parties to discover that the spouse is uninsurable or the cost of insurance is prohibitive.

Apply for a new policy solely for the purpose of insuring support. Although paying spouses may have coverage through their employment, if they leave their job or are terminated, the policy premium will be much more expensive to maintain because it is no longer priced at a group rate.

The payee should own the policy, if possible, and the payor is the insured. The beneficiary can be a trust for the children or, for spousal support, name the recipient of support directly. If the payee owns the policy, then they will be notified if it is at risk of lapsing or if the beneficiaries have been changed. The paying spouse will pay the premium to maintain the policy, but the spouse receiving support will own it. (This is also an estate planning strategy that keeps the death benefit out of the estate of the deceased.)

Use your divorce agreement to protect against lapses and changes to life insurance. Your divorce agreement can make clear that if the life insurance policy is not in place when the payor dies, then the payee has a claim against the paying spouse's estate for the amount of the death benefit. This will protect you as the recipient of support if the policy has lapsed or the beneficiaries have been changed without your knowledge.

Include a provision in your agreement for annual review of the policy. Add language to the agreement that specifies that the paying spouse must produce the policy and list of beneficiaries at least once a year to prove that the policy is in effect and the beneficiaries remain in place as stipulated in the divorce agreement.

QUESTIONS ABOUT SUPPORT FOR YOUR LAWYER

If I am entitled to both child support and spousal support, what is the best way to structure the income stream?

Are there advantages or disadvantages to taking spousal support instead of child support?

If I do an alimony buyout, can my ex come back and ask for support in the future?

What happens if my ex mismanages the buyout money?

What are my lifestyle restrictions when I'm receiving spousal support?

What happens if my ex dies before the support terminates and they are uninsured?

What happens if my ex failed to pay the premiums on the life insurance and it lapsed? What is my recourse?

QUESTIONS ABOUT SUPPORT FOR YOUR FINANCIAL ADVISOR

What is the net present value for my spousal support obligation?

Can I structure my portfolio/savings/retirement funds to produce income to pay my support obligations?

Can I afford to fund my alimony buyout?

What is the impact of an alimony buyout to my retirement plans?

How do I manage the lump-sum payment to provide for my future?

How much life insurance do I need?

Negotiating an Agreement for Your Marital Home

There is no single "best way" to divide the equity in your home. There are several options to consider, based on your circumstances.

SELL AS PART OF YOUR DIVORCE

If neither you nor your spouse wants or can afford to stay in your marital home, you can decide to sell the house and split the proceeds in your divorce. Depending on your circumstances, this option has several potential advantages. Selling gives everyone a fresh start—both you and your spouse get to move out and establish a new sense of home in keeping with your new family life. Presuming there is equity in your home, selling frees up cash for you to use to purchase (or rent) a new home that fits your budget and your new lifestyle. And you may be able to use some of the proceeds to strengthen your long-term financial security by adding to your investment or retirement accounts or funding your children's education savings accounts.

> ✔ **DO** confirm ahead of time that you will qualify for a mortgage on your own if you want to buy a new home after selling your current home in your divorce.

★ *Gabrielle's Pro Tip* If you are planning to move as part of your divorce, consider renting for at least a year to give yourself time to consider your options before you buy. You may find that you enjoy being free of the responsibility of home ownership.

By selling as part of your divorce, you can take maximum advantage of the capital gains tax exemption. If your home has appreciated in value since you purchased it, then whenever you sell, you will have to pay taxes on the *net gains*, which are gains or profits after paying expenses such as real estate commissions, last-minute repairs, and other expenses to prepare the house for the sale. If you sell the house while you're still married, you and your spouse are entitled to up to a $500,000 capital gains exemption, meaning you won't be taxed on up to $500,000 of the taxable increase in value during your ownership. If one of you keeps the home, your individual capital gains tax exemption will be $250,000 when you sell on your own. Whether married or single, to qualify for the capital gains tax exemption, your home must have been your primary residence for two of the previous five years.

If you (or your spouse) have decided that you want the house and can afford it, what are your options?

CONSIDER A BUYOUT

You can buy your spouse out of their half of the equity in the house as part of your divorce agreement. To fund the buyout, you can use cash (often through refinancing the mortgage) or exchange other marital assets for your spouse's share of the equity in your home. You can agree to take less of another asset—for example, you keep their share of the home equity and they keep an equal amount from the investments or savings accounts—or you can divide all your assets in half and then provide your spouse with their share of the equity in your home from your half. Ask your financial advisor or CPA which buyout option is more advantageous for your financial circumstances.

It is important to be aware that under most circumstances, a buyout may eventually require you to refinance your mortgage to remove your spouse from the mortgage. (You may also need to refinance to generate the cash to purchase your spouse's equity.) To refinance, you will need a good credit score and the income to qualify for the mortgage on your own.

🔥 *Red Flag* If your spouse is buying you out of your marital home, be sure you are removed from the mortgage at the time of your divorce. You don't want to be responsible for the debt without having the benefit of the asset. If you are not removed, you may risk your good credit if your ex fails to make all their payments on time for the remaining term of the mortgage. Most agreements will include a clause that indemnifies you in the event your spouse stops paying the loan. If you remain on the loan after a buyout, you may also have a tougher time qualifying for an additional mortgage of your own when you decide to purchase a home.

Ask yourself:

- *Do you have the funds for a buyout?*
- *Do you have significant appreciation in the home?*
- *Have you considered the tax consequences of selling the house yourself in the future?*

Remember, for individuals, the capital gains tax exemption is $250,000. If you have over $250,000 in capital gains (the increase in value since you bought the home), you will be solely responsible for paying the capital gains tax liability arising from the sale when you report the transaction on your income tax return.

✔ **DO** have the house appraised by a professional, divorce-trained home appraiser if you are considering a buyout.

✖ **DON'T** rely on a real estate agent's assessment based on comparable properties, an old appraisal, online "zestimates," or your city or town real estate tax assessment.

When to Seek a Valuation of Your Marital Home

If you and your spouse agree to sell the home, then it doesn't need to be professionally appraised. The market will determine its value. Whether you're the purchaser or seller, if you are considering a buyout, you will need to have your home appraised. Ideally, you and your spouse will come to an agreement up front about the appraiser you'll use. This will reduce mistrust around the value being too high or too low due to the appraiser's bias toward one spouse. If one of you disagrees with the appraised value, get a second opinion from a different appraiser. Even experienced appraisers can sometimes miss valuable details about the home, especially in a busy market.

✔ **DO** hire an appraiser who is specifically trained for divorce purposes.

✖ **DON'T** rely on the opinion of a real estate agent for valuation purposes.

✖ **DON'T** hire another appraiser for a second opinion without consulting your spouse. You will spend money, and the appraisal will not be useful if your spouse didn't agree to the second valuation.

CONSIDER JOINT OWNERSHIP

This option isn't for everyone, and it carries risk because it leaves you financially tied to your spouse. But under certain circumstances, it may be worth considering.

Blake was a client of mine whose two children were in their last few years of high school at the time of the divorce. Blake didn't want to keep the house long-term but also didn't want the kids to have to move and potentially change schools. The couple decided to maintain joint ownership until their kids went to college. They structured a specific provision in their divorce agreement that stipulated each spouse's responsibility for home expenses, outlined how they would handle property tax deductions, and set a clear time frame for when they would put the house on the market.

If the house isn't your forever home and you expect to move within three to five years, then it may be worth considering joint ownership so you don't need to move twice. There are a couple of ways to approach joint home ownership, depending on how cooperative you and your spouse are and your respective financial circumstances:

- Freeze the value of the house now and pay your spouse their share from the proceeds when you sell. Provide a specific date to list the house for sale. If the market goes up, your ex only gets what they agreed to, plus interest. Same if the house goes down in value—you pay your ex what you agreed to pay, plus interest.

- Maintain joint ownership and one of you lives in it, paying the expenses as a "renter." Under this arrangement, the spouse living in the home often pays for the utilities and routine maintenance expenses such as snow removal and lawn care, while the nonresident spouse pays the mortgage, taxes, and home insurance. Home repair expenses can be split, and repair costs over a certain predetermined amount (e.g., $100, $250, $500) should be agreed to in advance of hiring someone. If only one of you has the funds to pay for repairs, then that owner would be reimbursed upon the sale of the home. Reimbursements come "off the top" of the proceeds before the remainder is split according to the agreement.

> ✘ **DON'T** overlook tax considerations in a joint ownership arrangement. If you and your spouse decide to own your home jointly for a period after your divorce, be clear in your divorce agreement about which spouse will take the real estate tax and mortgage interest deduction on their personal income taxes.

✔ **DO** be realistic with yourself about whether this arrangement will work. Joint ownership requires a lot of cooperation and communication. No matter how cooperative and amicable you and your spouse are, to make this work you need to put everything in writing up front as part of your divorce agreement.

QUESTIONS FOR YOUR LAWYER

How do I change the deed to the house?

Can my ex be on the mortgage but not the deed?

We bought the home together; does it matter who is on the deed?

Does it matter if one of us vacates the house during the divorce process?

QUESTIONS FOR YOUR FINANCIAL ADVISOR

Can I afford to stay in my home?

How much does it cost to operate the home?

What are the projected capital gains on the house?

Can I refinance the mortgage? What if interest rates have increased?

What are my options for buying out my spouse if I don't qualify for a refinance?

Will I be on the mortgage even though my ex keeps the house?

How can I get removed from the mortgage without refinancing?

Are there any tax benefits to keeping/selling the house now?

Negotiating a Division of Your Investment Portfolios

If your marital assets include brokerage accounts or other taxable investment accounts—stocks, bonds, mutual funds, index funds, commodities, hedge funds—you have two main options to consider in dividing these assets in your divorce:

DIVIDE ASSETS IN-KIND. Assets divided in-kind means that the mutual fund shares, or shares of stock, are not sold and are instead divided between you and your spouse. If you have 1,000 shares of Apple stock purchased during your marriage, you each get 500 shares. If you have 1,001 shares, you each get 500 shares and the odd share is sold and the proceeds divided. If you're taking this route, talk with your divorce financial advisor or accountant about the tax consequences of dividing investments in-kind.

SELL AND SPLIT THE PROCEEDS. You and your spouse can agree to sell those 1,000 shares of Apple and divide the proceeds equitably between you. Making informed decisions about whether to divide in-kind or sell and split depends on your understanding of several factors, including:

- The current and projected value of the investments

- How holding or selling these assets will affect your cash flow

- The tax consequences associated with whether—and when—you sell

> ✔ **DO** collect three years of tax forms and portfolio statements (or better yet, year-end reports) from all financial institutions as you prepare to negotiate a division of your investments.

This is an area where your certified divorce financial advisor and your accountant can be of tremendous help to you, assisting you in analyzing the value of the assets that you are considering splitting, keeping, selling, or transferring to your spouse. Taking into consideration the specific investments you hold, your cash flow picture, and the tax consequences of your options, your financial advisor can advise you on which assets to keep and which to liquidate or transfer.

✔ **DO** engage the services of a certified divorce financial advisor or CPA to make tax-related investment decisions.

There are some fundamental considerations that every client needs to take into account when thinking about dividing nonretirement investments.

HOW INVESTMENTS FIT INTO YOUR CASH FLOW. Having a strong sense of what your cash flow needs are and how these investments support that plan is critical at this point in your decision-making. Stocks produce dividends, which is cash for you. Before you sell or agree to transfer any asset, look at the different types of value that it may offer you: How will keeping, selling, or transferring any given asset affect your current income? How does holding, selling, or transferring the asset affect your long-term financial plan?

✔ **DO** make sure you are working with a licensed investment advisor with significant experience in divorce. And if you haven't yet had your financial advisor do a cash flow analysis, do that now, before you agree to sell or transfer investment assets.

YOUR CAPITAL GAINS EXPOSURE. Although cash is king, one critical caveat around selling investment holdings in nonretirement accounts is the capital gains tax. Before you decide to sell, you must calculate the capital gains and be prepared to put funds away to pay this tax liability in the following year. When you pay capital gains, you will end up with fewer dollars in your pocket. Be sure to check with your divorce financial advisor or your accountant before agreeing to sell any assets. There are a couple of important things to know about capital gains:

- You can offset capital gains by selling investments that carry a capital loss. Remember, capital gains tax is a tax on the increase in value of the investment from the time you purchased it to the time of the sale. When you sell investment holdings that have lost value since you purchased them, you can claim a capital loss deduction for the decrease in value. The capital loss deduction can reduce your capital gains tax. There is a limit to how much capital loss you can deduct. But if you have more capital losses than you can claim in a single tax year, you can carry these losses over to future tax years.

- How long you've owned the assets determines how your capital gains will be taxed. If you have held shares in stock or other investments for less than one year at the time you sell them, the gains will be taxed at your ordinary income tax rates. If you have owned an investment for more than one year, you will pay capital gains tax rates when you sell. For many people—not all, but many—the capital gains tax rate may be lower than your income tax rate, but be sure to consult with your divorce financial advisor and/or accountant before you sell.

🔥 *Red Flag* Be sure to carefully review the investments that your spouse is offering to you if the offer is anything other than an in-kind, 50-50 split. Some stock holdings carry large capital gains tax liability, whereas other stock positions carry lower tax consequences if you sell them. It is best to consult with an investment professional to assist you in understanding what implications the trade carries for you and if you are at a disadvantage.

Once your investments have been divided, you must continue to analyze them to evaluate how well they continue to serve your financial goals. Working with a knowledgeable professional will help you understand the role of investments with respect to your financial goals. (In

Chapter 9, I talk about how to begin to develop your long-term financial plan after your divorce is final.)

QUESTIONS FOR YOUR LAWYER

Does it matter which investments I choose?

Will our collectibles be valued and treated differently from investment assets?

What if I lose money in the market after the divorce?

What if the value of the assets decreases before the assets are divided? What if it increases?

QUESTIONS FOR YOUR FINANCIAL ADVISOR

What are the tax implications of the proposed settlement?

Should I take all of one investment position and my spouse can take another?

Will these investments produce income for me?

Should I sell the stock positions that I get and spend the money?

How do these investments support my long-term financial goals?

How much does it cost to sell investments?

★ *Gabrielle's Pro Tip* Life insurance you or your spouse took out during your marriage may be an asset in your divorce. Some types of life insurance carry a valuable investment component and/or have cash value built into the policy. *The cash value of life insurance may be an asset to divide in your settlement.* You can also consider using the cash value of life insurance to fund the policy, which can keep the insurance policy up to date without tapping into cash flow.

Negotiating a Division of Your Retirement Assets

If you or your spouse contributed to retirement accounts during your marriage, those funds will generally be considered marital property, and you each are entitled to a fair share of them in your divorce settlement. Perhaps your spouse has made regular contributions to a 401(k) plan at work or has a pension plan through their employer. You and your spouse may have contributed to IRAs at times throughout your marriage. Whatever retirement assets you or your spouse generated during your married life, they need to be valued and divided in your divorce settlement.

Consult with a certified divorce financial advisor or CPA if you are considering taking a smaller share of retirement assets in exchange for a larger share of nonretirement assets. Your financial advisor can assess your overall asset mix and cash flow, project your future financial needs and the future value of the share of the retirement funds you are entitled to, and make sure you are agreeing to a fair deal that serves you over the long term.

★ *Gabrielle's Pro Tip* Contributions to retirement accounts made before your marriage may be considered separate property and exempt from division in a divorce. But, depending on the property laws in your state, any increase in value of these retirement funds that occurred during your marriage may be considered marital property, and you may be entitled to a fair share of those gains.

Also consult with a certified divorce financial advisor if you or your spouse has a pension through work. Dividing a pension relies, in part, on a projection of the pension's future value. Valuation of a pension is complicated and best conducted by a valuation specialist. Your financial advisor can assist you with coordinating the valuation, hiring a specialist, and assessing the value of other retirement assets in your marital estate.

There is a distinction in retirement plans that is important to understand as you prepare to divide your retirement assets in your divorce.

Qualified plans are retirement plans that are protected from creditors by the federal government through the Employee Retirement Income Security Act of 1974 (ERISA). In a divorce, assets in a qualified plan that are subject to division will require a Qualified Domestic Relations Order, or QDRO. Pensions and 401(k) and 403(b) plans are all qualified retirement plans. IRAs are *not* qualified plans. State property laws regulate how nonqualified plans are divided in a divorce.

A QDRO (pronounced "quad-ro") is a court order to a qualified retirement plan administrator instructing them *how, when,* and *how much* to divide and transfer from one spouse's employer-based qualified retirement account to the other spouse in a divorce.

QDROs must comply with both federal and state law since ERISA is a federal law and divorce law is state-specific. The US Department of Labor (*www.dol.org*) provides detailed information on dividing retirement benefits using QDROs.

The QDRO is a protracted, complex, technical process that can take months to complete. The process involves six steps:

1. A QDRO specialist drafts the document setting forth the division of assets as stipulated in the divorce agreement. *The QDRO document is plan-specific and must include the information and format that your employer plan requires.*

2. If your plan requires prefiling approval, the QDRO specialist will submit a draft document to the plan administrator for review.

3. If approved, the QDRO specialist will then submit the preapproved QDRO and supporting documentation to the court in the jurisdiction where your divorce case was heard.

4. The court will approve, sign, and certify the QDRO and return it to the specialist.

5. The specialist will send the approved QDRO to the employee plan administrator for processing.

6. The plan administrator will confirm receipt, request information about the ex-spouse who is receiving the funds, and open an account for the funds to be transferred to that ex-spouse.

★ *Gabrielle's Pro Tip* Plan administrators are busy and overwhelmed with QDROs. Be sure to ask the specialist or your attorney to follow up to confirm that they received the QDRO.

⭐ **NOTE** The ex-spouse who is receiving the funds has options for what comes next. You can roll the funds over to your own IRA, transfer them to your 401(k) at your current employer, or take a taxable distribution. If the recipient of funds is age 59½ or older, a 10 percent early withdrawal penalty will not be assessed. If the recipient is younger than age 59½, you can take advantage of an underused option in the QDRO process. If you are receiving retirement funds in a QDRO transfer, you can take a distribution directly from the plan at the time of the transfer without incurring the IRS's 10 percent early withdrawal penalty. Rather than rolling over the funds to an IRA, you would have the money moved directly from the new 401(k) to a nonretirement account, such as a checking, savings, or money market account. Bear in mind, you will still be required to pay income tax on these funds by reporting the distribution on your income tax return for that year.

The process of drafting the QDRO documents and filing them with the court is performed by specialists. Your attorney will likely not be drafting a QDRO. To avoid unnecessary delays, if your divorce settlement includes one or more QDROs, be sure that your agreement does the following:

- Names the preferred QDRO specialist you will use for the process
- Specifies who will pay the fees (typically $300-1,000); these are usually split 50-50
- Sets a deadline for when the QDRO process will be initiated or a QDRO specialist hired

The QDRO process is time-consuming, complicated, and expensive. *In some cases, divorcing spouses will have enough assets in IRAs to fund an equitable division of retirement assets, and they can avoid the QDRO process altogether.* But not everyone has enough in other retirement funds to do so.

If you anticipate you will use a QDRO to receive funds from your ex-spouse's retirement accounts, talk with your attorney about arranging to have the funds taken out of investments and held in cash while the QDRO process works through the system in order to protect the value of the asset from changes in the market. A now-client of mine, Sherry, lost several hundred thousand dollars while waiting for a QDRO to be completed. Sherry is a new client who came to me after her divorce was finalized and her QDRO completed. At the time of Sherry's divorce, her share of her spouse's qualified retirement funds was $2.25 million. Because of market volatility and the time it took to complete the QDRO, when she received her portion of her ex-spouse's employer-based retirement funds, her share was worth $1.5 million. Had Sherry and her attorney requested that the retirement funds be protected in cash while the QDRO process played out, she would have received the amount she anticipated. If you or your spouse has left behind a qualified plan, such as a 401(k) or 403(b), at a former employer, consider rolling those funds over to an IRA and then dividing the funds without using a QDRO. IRAs are not qualified plans. They can be divided by completing a simple form, signed by you and your spouse, and the funds can be transferred in-kind or in cash within thirty days. It's a faster, simpler, less expensive process than the QDRO. Don't overlook qualified plans from previous employers when preparing to divide your retirement assets.

Tax Basics for Dividing Retirement Benefits

When dividing and transferring retirement assets, there is no tax consequence to either party if the funds are staying in retirement accounts. An IRA-IRA transfer from one spouse to another is not a taxable event. A QDRO transfer—for example, when funds are first moved from one 401(k) to another 401(k) and then rolled over to an IRA—is not a taxable event. Taxes are incurred only when a distribution is made from a retirement account into a nonretirement account. This is necessary at times in a divorce, and when it happens, you and your financial advisor can calculate the projected taxes and make a plan to pay them from your available assets.

SOCIAL SECURITY

You and your spouse will not divide Social Security benefits in your divorce. If, at the time your divorce is final, you had been married for at least ten years and you have been divorced at least two years when you file a claim, then at retirement age you will be entitled to either 50 percent of your spouse's Social Security benefit or 100 percent of your own Social Security benefit, but not both. You must choose one or the other benefit option. To receive 50 percent of your ex-spouse's Social Security benefit, you must also be unmarried when you are eligible to apply.

If your spouse claims a 50 percent share of your Social Security benefits, your benefit will not decrease. You will receive all the Social Security benefits you're entitled to, based on your contributions over your years of working, and the age at which you decide to begin drawing on Social Security. Visit *www.ssa.gov* to obtain your Social Security benefits record. The report will provide helpful information about what to expect for Social Security payments when you are eligible to apply.

★ *Gabrielle's Pro Tip* Dividing retirement assets can be complex. In addition to ERISA and non-ERISA plans, veterans' retirement benefits and federal/state/county/municipal employee retirement benefit plans can have their own specific requirements for how they may be split in a divorce. Work carefully with your lawyer and financial advisor to identify all the retirement assets in your marital estate, and to make sure your divorce agreement complies with the rules of division for these assets before you sign a final agreement.

DIVIDING IRAS

State law regulates the division and transfer of individual retirement account (IRA) funds. There are a couple of main options to consider in dividing these funds:

AGREE TO A ROLLOVER. At the account holder's direction, their spouse's share of the retirement assets can be withdrawn (with no penalty or tax to the account holder), with the funds distributed directly to the recipient spouse. The recipient will have a limited, specified amount of time to deposit the funds into another retirement account, typically sixty days. If the IRA funds remain in a nonretirement account, the recipient will have to report the distribution on their tax return and pay taxes on the money as income, and perhaps pay the additional 10 percent penalty for early withdrawal of retirement assets if they are younger than 59½.

AGREE TO A DIRECT TRANSFER. Also known as a trustee to trustee transfer, this arrangement moves the agreed-upon share of one spouse's IRA funds to another IRA account in the recipient's name. If you anticipate receiving IRA funds from your spouse in your divorce, consider setting up an IRA at the same financial institution where your spouse's IRA resides. This will likely speed up the process, and you'll have your money sooner. You can move the money to a different financial institution later if you choose.

Before you agree in writing to a settlement, make sure the directions for dividing all IRAs are specifically outlined in the agreement, including the amount to be transferred, how and when the transfer will be executed, and account details (including account numbers) for each IRA involved.

QUESTIONS FOR YOUR LAWYER

How will the QDROs be drafted?

How long will it take to get my funds from my spouse's 401(k)?

How much does a QDRO cost?

Who pays for the QDRO to be prepared?

What if I have more in retirement funds than my spouse? I was a saver, but my spouse spent and never made contributions to a retirement account—do I have to share mine?

Am I entitled to my spouse's Social Security benefit?

QUESTIONS FOR YOUR FINANCIAL ADVISOR

How much money will I need for retirement?

Does it matter if I take retirement funds instead of nonretirement funds from our asset division?

What are the taxes if I take a distribution from a retirement account before age 59½?

When do I pay the taxes?

Can I contribute to retirement funds if I am getting alimony and child support?

Does it make a difference if I take funds from a 401(k) versus an IRA?

Is my Social Security taxable income?

Can I work and still receive Social Security benefits?

Negotiating a Division of Your Debts

Addressing debt is an often-neglected component of separating marital finances during divorce, and failing to come up with a plan for your debts now can lead to painful and costly financial headaches long after your divorce is final. Nobody wants to think about debt; it's stressful and can be confusing. But your long-term financial security depends on addressing your marital debts now as comprehensively as you can. Take a deep breath and focus on these priorities as you work through negotiations and toward a settlement.

KNOW EXACTLY WHICH DEBTS ARE YOUR RESPONSIBILITY

To come to a fair agreement in your settlement, you need a crystal-clear understanding of all the debts you share with your spouse (marital debt), as well as debt that belongs to you alone. As part of completing your financial statement, you identified your personal debts and shared debts that you and your spouse generated during your marriage. You also need to pay close and careful attention to identifying who is responsible for debts incurred while your divorce is in progress.

Remember, debts accrued during a marriage are typically a joint liability: both you and your spouse are responsible, regardless of whose name is on the account. During your divorce, your liability for your spouse's debts will depend largely on *when* debts are generated and *what* the funds were used for.

First, the *when*. Your state's date of separation is key here. Debts generated after your legal separation date will generally belong to you and your spouse individually. Depending on the laws of your state, that might be as early as when one of you informed the other of your intent to divorce, or as late as the day your divorce is final. This is one reason it's so important to monitor your credit report and the activity in your financial accounts, so you remain keenly aware of how your spouse is spending money during your divorce and what new debts they are accumulating. Having this knowledge enables you to work toward a fair legal distribution of debt in your settlement.

Next, the *what*. The debts you and your spouse incur during your divorce to support your household and your children will generally be regarded by the court as your joint responsibility. If your spouse used a joint credit card to entertain a new person in their life or on activities that don't support the kids or the family, then it is likely that you won't be held responsible. (You will need to document their spending to avoid joint responsibility for these debts, however.) If you have a home equity line of credit (HELOC) against your marital home, how were these funds spent during your divorce? If you or your spouse used the money to support your household and family—paying college expenses, buying a car, making home improvements—then this debt will likely be shared between you in your divorce settlement. But if your spouse used the funds for other reasons—such as for vacations with a new partner, or their attorney's fees—then it will likely be considered their debt to repay.

★ *Gabrielle's Pro Tip* If you or your spouse has federal or state income tax debt, you may be jointly responsible for those tax debts throughout your marriage and separation. If you signed a tax return with your spouse and a tax bill is due, the IRS can hold you responsible for paying the entire bill. Be sure to work closely with your attorney and your accountant on addressing tax liabilities during your divorce.

ELIMINATE AS MUCH SHARED DEBT AS POSSIBLE

After you're divorced, you will have no control over what your spouse does with their money. If they fail to honor a commitment to pay off a debt that you are connected to, that will impact your credit score, affecting your ability to buy a home, finance a car, and get new credit cards. Once divorced, you will have little recourse to recover funds from them if they fail to pay, and it will certainly impact your relationship with them.

PAY OFF AS MUCH MARITAL DEBT AS YOU CAN AS PART OF YOUR SETTLEMENT. To the extent you and your spouse can pay down your marital debt at the time of your divorce, you will minimize your financial risks in the next chapter of your life. You'll also reduce your expenses and probably improve your credit score, both of significant benefit to you as you establish your post-divorce financial life. Paying off a mortgage or home equity line of credit is easily done when the home is sold. You can consider using the proceeds of selling your home to pay off joint credit card debts or debt you owe to taxing authorities (IRS or your state).

★ *Gabrielle's Pro Tip* If you and your spouse agree, you can pay off high interest credit cards with a home equity line of credit. This is an option to consider if you intend to sell the home jointly in the next two to three years. Take note, however: this strategy is not advisable if the HELOC interest rate is higher than your current mortgage. And HELOCs typically carry a variable rate, so if interest rates increase (or decrease), your payments will adjust accordingly.

PROTECT YOURSELF FROM THE MARITAL DEBT THAT REMAINS AFTER YOUR DIVORCE. If you can't pay off your marital debts with marital assets at the time of your divorce, responsibility for paying these debts will be divided between you and your spouse in your settlement agreement. There are steps you may be able to take to protect yourself from one day being liable for the marital debt your spouse will be responsible for after your divorce.

REFINANCE EXISTING LOANS TO REMOVE YOURSELF (OR YOUR SPOUSE) FROM THE LOAN. If your spouse is keeping the house or a car with a loan, if possible have them refinance to remove you from the mortgage or loan. Ideally, the interest rate that they are refinancing into is lower than the one they have, and their monthly payment will be lower. However, if your spouse doesn't have a job or hasn't been receiving a consistent stream of support payments, they may not qualify.

TRANSFER REMAINING BALANCES FROM JOINT CREDIT CARDS TO INDIVIDUAL CARDS. As part of your settlement, you and your spouse will need to close any joint credit cards and come to an agreement on how you will share the responsibility for paying off those balances. You can transfer your shares of debt to individual cards and pay off balances over time, or pay them out of your share of marital assets after your divorce is final.

SET UP A PAYMENT PLAN WITH THE IRS. If you and your spouse are responsible for tax debt, make a payment plan with the IRS (or your state taxation agency, for state tax debt) before your divorce is final.

MAKE AUTOMATIC PAYMENTS PART OF YOUR DIVORCE AGREEMENT. If your settlement agreement stipulates that your spouse will make payments on a debt that you're legally liable for, make automatic payment on this debt a requirement in writing in your settlement.

QUESTIONS FOR YOUR LAWYER

How do the divorce laws in my state treat marital debt?

How long I am legally responsible for the debts my spouse generates?

Am I responsible for credit card bills my spouse used to buy their girl/ boyfriend gifts before we separated?

What are the debts that am I legally bound to split with my spouse?

What debts are my individual responsibility?

What debts are my spouse's individual responsibility? Can I be held legally liable for these debts if my spouse fails to pay them after the divorce?

QUESTIONS FOR YOUR FINANCIAL ADVISOR

Looking at all my debts and assets, is there a way to pay off what I owe with a lower interest rate and payment?

How do I create a payment plan with the IRS?

Should I sell my house to pay off debt?

If I sell the house, what are the expected proceeds and should I use them to pay off my credit cards?

How do I remove my spouse from my credit cards?

Mediation wasn't easy for Vita and Taylor, but they made it work. The parenting schedule took some time to settle, and tempers flared at times as the spouses sought an arrangement that gave their kids a consistent routine and time with both parents and enabled both Taylor and Vita to work. They agreed to a 50-50 split of parenting time, with a carve-out for Taylor's work travel. After a lot of back-and-forth, Vita and Taylor agreed that Vita would take on the extra time with the kids when Taylor was out of town, and that Taylor would give her three days' notice ahead of any travel. "It used to drive me nuts when Taylor came home and dropped the news, like, offhand, about leaving town for work the very next day," Vita told me. She felt their arrangement, with a clear provision for advance notice, could actually make things easier than when they were living under the same roof, provided Taylor lived up to the agreement. "I have the flexibility in my work that Taylor doesn't," she said. "I can pivot to more time with the kids." The provision for notice was important for her to be able to plan to change her schedule, she said, and it also codified the respect and consideration for her time that she felt had been lacking in the later years of her marriage.

With their parenting plan worked out, the spouses used their state's child support calculator to establish a monthly child support amount that Taylor would pay Vita. Because of the duration of their marriage and the disparity in their incomes, Vita was entitled to spousal support, which they agreed Taylor would pay in a lump-sum amount at the time of their divorce. Vita and I worked on a financial plan and budget that would use her spousal support funds as income over time, while she gradually built up her client base for her graphic design company. She and Taylor agreed to a provision in their settlement that said Taylor would not return to court to request a change in child support as Vita's income increased, up to $25,000 a year. This provision gave Vita a clear path to work more as she was able. It also increased her ability to plan and budget for the next few years. And it gave her peace of mind that she sorely needed.

Given that Vita and Taylor had no financial resources when they got married, they tallied up their retirement, checking, and savings accounts and divided them equally. Deciding what to do with the house took some time. They debated owning it jointly for a few years before ultimately agreeing to sell. The market had risen quite a bit since they purchased the home, and there was enough equity to split to help them both buy in a less expensive town that was closer to Taylor's office and to Vita's sister and family. Taylor planned to keep renting for a year before buying, but Vita was moving ahead quickly with a search for a new home so the kids wouldn't have to do multiple moves. Vita was excited for the change. "We'll definitely have 'less house,' but it will be fun to set up a new space and the kids are already excited about designing their new rooms."

Vita and Taylor were currently reviewing a draft of a final agreement with their lawyers, and Vita and I were going over the numbers in her budget again, comparing them against the support numbers in the draft agreement. They hadn't quite crossed the finish line, but they were close and on their way. And I could already see Vita seemed lighter, quicker to laugh and smile, ready to move into her new chapter. "I'm not done being sad," she said. "I'm not sure I'll ever be totally done. But I like where I'm headed."

Key Takeaways and Next Steps

- You are your own best and most important advocate in your divorce. Your ability to work as an informed, focused participant in your divorce negotiations is critical to getting a final agreement that meets your needs and serves your interests. It's hard work and it's worth the effort.

- Be thorough and deliberate in thinking about all the components of your financial settlement. Pay close attention to details.

- Be in regular contact with your attorney and financial advisor. Ask questions whenever you don't understand something and speak up anytime something doesn't feel right to you.

- Don't rely on your attorney to make financial calculations or conduct financial analysis in your case. Discuss the financial components of your settlement negotiations with a qualified divorce financial advisor and a CPA.

CHAPTER SEVEN

Thinking Your Way Strategically Through Negotiation to an Agreement

Maintaining perspective in divorce is hard work. To negotiate effectively, you need to accept that the process is a business deal and think logically, even as you are riding an emotional roller coaster. Throughout your divorce, you must pay close attention to details but not get stuck in the weeds. Rather, you will use your command of the details to achieve your big-picture goal: a divorce agreement that protects you financially and serves your future financial interests. You may be emotionally caught up in *what happened*, but your focus needs to be on *what can be*. Divorce is a path to the future, not an accounting of the past.

Keeping perspective and staying rational can feel like a high-wire balancing act. The emotional journey of divorce makes it all too easy to act out of spite, revenge, jealousy, or a desire to control. It is understandable that you may feel scared or angry, or want to punish your spouse in your divorce. But stepping back and acting out of reason is the best way to stay out of court and get your divorce resolved as quickly, inexpensively, and successfully as possible.

How to Run a Holistic Cost-Benefit Analysis for Nearly Every Decision in Your Divorce

Nobody reaches a final divorce agreement without compromise. You've created a vision of your future and a financial budget that outlines your financial needs, hopes, and dreams. Together, they provide an important framework for analyzing and evaluating offers from your spouse. A cost-benefit analysis will help you bridge the gap between your vision and needs and the reality of a settlement proposal you must consider.

A meaningful cost-benefit analysis isn't a dry computation of numbers—though the numbers are extremely important. A true, holistic cost-benefit analysis considers not only the value of marital assets and support at stake, but also the emotional impact, time and effort, and additional costs of settling, continuing to negotiate, or—worst case—going to court to have a judge decide. You can use this decision-making framework throughout your divorce regardless of the approach you're taking, and you can apply it to nearly every decision you will make. In negotiations, it can help you decide when (and how much) to compromise, when to hold firm, and when to fight for more. In reviewing settlement offers, it can help you determine whether what's being offered to you meets your needs financially, emotionally, and in terms of your peace of mind. It can help you to navigate communicating with your spouse inside and outside the negotiation room. A holistic cost-benefit analysis will keep you connected to your goals and vision. It will keep you in touch with your emotions so you are managing them, rather than having them manage you. It can give you a sense of control and ownership over your decision-making when it otherwise can feel like you are spiraling downward, confused and grasping in the dark.

WHAT DO I WANT?

You will be asked what you want throughout your divorce process. Your attorney will ask, your friends will ask, and your spouse will ask. You will face countless choices and decisions throughout your divorce. Every time you encounter a decision, the first step in your process is to be clear about your goal and what outcome you are seeking from the choice at hand. Do you want the house, the "fun" car, or the oil painting by that up-and-coming artist? Do you want to keep your spouse from getting a share of the equity in your new business venture? Do you want financial redress for your spouse's reckless or improper spending during your separation? Do you want your higher-earning spouse to pay school tuition and summer camp fees? You can't start the process of making an informed choice without first being clear and specific about what it is you want. What, exactly, is the puzzle piece you're working with?

> ✖ **DON'T** underestimate how much money you can spend during your divorce on things that will be rendered meaningless or unimportant in your next chapter.

WHY DO I WANT THIS?

The *why* underlying your goals is every bit as important as the *what*. Before you act, make a decision, or commit to or reject an offer, be clear and honest with yourself about why you are seeking a particular outcome. Do you want the "fun" car because it's the most suitable for your morning commute—or because your spouse loves it and you want to keep them from enjoying it? Do you want information about who your spouse is seeing because you are worried they are using marital assets to fund a new relationship—or because it's driving you crazy not to know how they are spending their time, and with whom?

Your emotions are going to be running high, understandably so. And acting before you know *why* you're doing so can escalate conflict and lead you to make decisions that may not serve your big-picture best interests. As you work through decisions related to your divorce, be unflinchingly honest with yourself about what is motivating you, and do it without self-judgment. There are no wrong answers. What matters is that you gain clarity about your motivation before you move forward with your cost-benefit analysis. After you've factored in the financial and emotional costs, you may decide your *why* is worth it, or you may decide the costs are too steep. Taking time to understand your why provides you with valuable insight before you take action and can give you meaningful peace of mind when reflecting on your decisions in hindsight.

Over the years of their marriage, Susan and Sam enjoyed boating. Susan took care of arranging provisions for their excursions, and Sam took care of keeping the boat clean and maintained, charting the courses for their trips, and driving the boat. In their divorce, the boat became a point of contention. Susan knew how much Sam loved the boat. She did, too. Susan had great memories of their trips together. She couldn't stand the thought of Sam having the boat and taking trips with a new love. Despite not knowing how to drive it, Susan fought hard to keep the boat. Susan and Sam had the boat valued, and after much negotiation, it was agreed that Susan would keep the boat and buy Sam out of their half of the equity in the boat. It was only after the divorce, when she updated her budget, that Susan realized how expensive the boat was to store, maintain, and operate. She hadn't factored the boat expenses into her budget. Ultimately Susan sold the boat for less money than she gave Sam for their equity. Neither spouse got the boat, and no one was happy with the outcome. Susan lost money and Sam lost the boat. The mistake could have been avoided entirely had Susan taken the time to think through what was really motivating her and to play out the economic consequences of acting out of revenge rather than using her smart, savvy business sense.

✔ **DO** your financial homework. What do you have, what do you need, what can you let go of? Successful negotiators know when they can compromise and when they need to hold firm. That insight comes from a clear understanding of their financial circumstances.

WHAT IS THE FINANCIAL VALUE AT STAKE?

To make informed decisions in negotiations, you need to know your numbers. Before you decide to fight for an asset or an issue in your divorce, know the dollar value of what you are fighting for. What is the value of the oil painting you've got your heart set on? What is the share of the business your spouse is offering you worth today, and what is its potential long-term value to you? Be precise in identifying the financial value of the asset or issue at stake in your decision. Your financial advisor can help you.

Remember, you're putting a whole puzzle together, and all the pieces are connected. After you've identified the stand-alone value of the asset in dispute, step back and consider how the asset you're seeking fits into the larger financial picture you are assembling. Ask yourself: *How will the puzzle change if I get what I want? What happens to the puzzle if I don't get what I want?* There are always trade-offs that need to be made in negotiating a divorce settlement. *What other piece of the puzzle might I need to give up or change in order to get what I want?*

> ✔ **DO** keep your financial statement updated as expenses and asset values change over time, and know the valuation dates that affect your divorce. Be sure you're working with accurate numbers when it's time to consider a settlement offer.

WHAT ARE THE FINANCIAL COSTS AT STAKE?

What will it cost to get what you want? When considering whether to compromise, hold firm, or fight for more, take into account the costs of your decision. These costs include legal fees and fees for other professionals and experts (forensic accountants, expert witnesses, private investigators, multiple valuation experts, etc.). Will fighting for this piece of the puzzle mean you're likely to go to trial rather than settle? Ask your lawyer to estimate for you the additional time they will need to put into your case to pursue your interest. Do your homework and develop an estimate of the costs of the additional professional help you may need to achieve what you want. Ask yourself: *Are the financial costs of what I'm seeking worth the potential gains? If I prevail, what will my actual, net financial gain be after I've paid the costs associated with "winning"?* Assemble your numbers, do the math, and give the financial bottom line in your decision a long, hard look.

> ✖ **DON'T** spend more money on lawyers fighting for items that aren't worth the cost of legal fees.

WHAT IS THE EMOTIONAL VALUE AT STAKE?

Peace of mind, a sense of security, an attachment to meaningful possessions, drawing boundaries that feel reasonable and right: the decisions you make throughout your divorce have emotional values. And your spouse has emotional value at stake in your decisions as well. The emotional benefits at stake aren't calculated in dollars, but you can assess them and consider them in tandem with the financial values attached to your choices. Ask yourself: *What are the core values and emotions at stake for me in this matter? What do I stand to gain emotionally from this choice? How will pursuing this goal help me heal and move forward with my life? Is this about strengthening my emotional well-being or about hurting my spouse?* Remember, all your emotions are valid. This isn't about judging the emotions wrapped up in your decision. It's about being aware of them and developing an understanding of how your actions—and their consequences—will help or hurt you in the bigger picture.

> Cam knows how much Tim enjoys cooking. As he and Tim are dividing up the contents of their home, Cam states that he wants the "good" knife. Cam knows that this knife is one of Tim's favorite tools. Cam also knows that he himself will never use it. Cam is seeking to take an item with emotional rather than financial value, which will inevitably cause Tim to react negatively. Cam and Tim will spend hours with their attorneys fighting over the knife, incurring fees and conflict, when clearly the knife is not worth what is being spent on fighting over who gets it. If

Cam had been honest with himself about why he was determined to have the knife (to punish Tim), and if he'd taken the time to assess the financial costs of fighting over the knife (far greater than the value of the knife itself), he'd likely have made a different decision, and their divorce would have proceeded more quickly, cost less, and been less charged with conflict and animosity.

✔ **DO** be efficient with your lawyer dollars. Think before picking up the phone or sending an email. Is this a question better suited for your financial advisor or an issue to discuss with your therapist?

WHAT ARE THE EMOTIONAL COSTS AT STAKE?

Contentious, high-conflict divorces are emotionally exhausting for everyone involved, particularly for children who, on top of adjusting to the fundamental changes in their family structure, also must endure their parents' ongoing acrimony. Stress, poor sleep, depression, and anxiety are just some of the real-life consequences of divorces that get ugly and drag on indefinitely. When making decisions throughout your divorce, consider the emotional impact on you, your children, your children's relationship with their other parent, and your own relationship with your ex in the future. There will be weddings, the arrival of grandchildren, holidays, graduations, and plenty of other occasions where you and your ex may be together. To what degree will a decision to fight for a larger share of assets prolong the divorce process and delay your family's ability to heal and start fresh?

It's important to keep in mind the emotional toll a legal fight will take on you and your children. I advise continuing to rely on your therapist for help. Your emotions will shift and change throughout your divorce. The initial shock, fear, and sadness may give way to frustration, anger, and resentment by the time you're deep into negotiations and considering settlement proposals. To negotiate and evaluate settlements effectively, you need to focus and set your emotions aside. Unpack your emotions with your therapist so they don't undermine you in your mediation session or your lawyer's office.

Jordan found a credit card charge for an expensive item at an out-of-state jewelry store. When Jordan asked her spouse about the charge, they claimed that it was for a luxury pen for their new office. Not convinced, Jordan called the store asking for a copy of the receipt for her records. The jewelry store emailed the receipt, and it confirmed Jordan's suspicions. The item her spouse purchased was not, in fact, a pen, but a bracelet. Jordan's attorney produced this document to her spouse's attorney, and Jordan was reimbursed for 50 percent of the purchase. Ultimately, the parties agreed on a lump-sum amount to cover the marital funds Jordan's spouse had spent on their new paramour.

Jordan could have spent the time, money, and energy to track down every last penny her spouse spent. But the legal fees were climbing, and the divorce was taking a toll on her mental health. For Jordan, the additional time and effort wasn't worth it. The parties agreed to a dollar amount to account for the improper spending, which allowed Jordan to move forward with the divorce process and more quickly into her new life, free of her spouse and on to a new, more positive chapter.

HOW LIKELY AM I TO BE SUCCESSFUL?

In negotiation, people are most effective when they have decided what they want and are realistic about whether they can get it. Before you take a position—like opting to fight for an asset or reject a compromise from your spouse—assess your chances of achieving your goal. Your attorney and your financial advisor can help you set realistic expectations about what success might look like and how likely you are to achieve it. Then it will be up to you to decide whether the chances of success are worth the financial and emotional costs.

Play out the different outcomes at stake in your decision and take the time to imagine the best-case and worst-case scenarios. Ask yourself: *How will I feel if I don't get what I want? How will I feel if I get a scaled-down version of what I'm hoping for? What middle-ground outcome (not best-case, not worst-case) would make it worth it to pursue my interest? How will achieving what I want affect my financial plans, budget, and cash flow? How will failing to get what I want affect my financial plans, budget, and cash flow?*

Using a Cost-Benefit Analysis to Help You Communicate with Your Spouse

You may be in frequent communication with your spouse throughout your divorce. Sometimes those communications may be structured, such as in a mediation session. You're also likely to be communicating in person, over the phone, and via text about your children, bills and expenses, and issues related to your case. Your communication with your spouse—within and beyond negotiations—will affect the emotional tenor of your divorce and your ability to work efficiently and effectively to strike the business deal that is your divorce agreement. You can't control your spouse's behavior and choices. But you can control your own. Being deliberate and intentional in your communications with your spouse puts you in a position of power and influence over the course your divorce takes. You can use a version of this holistic cost-benefit analysis to prepare for and manage your interactions with your spouse while you're working through your divorce. Ask yourself:

- *What do I want from this conversation? What is my goal?*
- *Why do I want this?*
- *What is the financial value at stake?*
- *What are the potential financial costs at stake?*
- *What are the potential outcomes—best case, worst case, most likely?*
- *What are the emotional benefits that could result?*
- *What are the emotional costs or risks that could result?*
- *How likely am I to be successful in getting what I want?*

- *Is it worth it?*

- *Is there another, more effective way to approach my spouse in order to get what I want?*

    You know your spouse like nobody else. You know their triggers, their background, and their history with money and family. The best negotiators know their opponent better than anyone and are disciplined about using this information to their advantage.

✔ **DON'T** hide money or tangible marital assets. This will cause mistrust and rack up legal fees. You will ultimately be required by the court to produce these assets. It's not worth it.

How to Evaluate a Settlement Offer from Your Spouse

Before you do anything regarding a settlement offer presented by your spouse, check in with yourself about your expectations. Be prepared for the reality that it will likely not contain everything—perhaps many things—that you want or expect. In the course of your divorce, a settlement proposal is not the end. It is, we hope, the *beginning* of the end. Expect there to be some back-and-forth before you get to a final agreement that you are ready to sign.

REVIEW THE ENTIRE PROPOSAL CAREFULLY WITH YOUR TEAM. In order to intelligently respond to the proposal, you must understand what is being presented to you. Review the proposal page by page, and then review it again. Use a highlighter to mark up any passages, phrases, words, or numbers that you don't understand. As you read, take notes and prepare questions to ask your attorney and financial advisor. Walk through the pages of the proposal with your attorney and financial advisor and ask yourself, Does this makes sense? Is this sustainable? Now is the time to bring up any questions with your team about details or terms that aren't clear to you. For every component of the proposal, ask your attorney and financial advisor to explain to you what the detailed, technical language means in plain English, and what its impact will be on your real life.

★ *Gabrielle's Pro Tip* All the legal language in front of you means something, even—and perhaps, especially—if it is boilerplate language. It takes discipline and vigilance not to mentally check out when reading legalese. Make sure you understand every line and every word of a proposed settlement in front of you.

CONSIDER THE PARENTING SCHEDULE. For people with young children, parenting schedules may be the first item on the proposal. Coordinating weekends, vacations, birthdays, and holidays is often less emotional than resolving financial issues. Remember, parenting time may also factor into child support calculations. Agreeing on a parenting schedule may allow you to calculate your child support income or outlay, which will make budgeting easier.

Ask yourself:

- *Is the routine schedule realistic and sustainable?*
- *Does it give me the time I need to work?*
- *Does it include clear plans for summer and school-year vacations, long weekends, holidays, and birthdays? For sick days? For accompanying our children to medical appointments, therapy, afterschool classes, and other obligations and activities?*
- *Are there contingency plans for when one of us needs to travel?*

BEGIN WITH A CAREFUL REVIEW OF THE FINANCIAL FUNDAMENTALS. Before you can intelligently analyze a settlement offer from your spouse, you need a clear understanding of what assets, debts, and income are being divided. And you should feel confident that the dollar values for all assets, debts, and income streams are accurate.

Ask yourself:

- *Do I agree with the overall inventory of assets?*
- *Do I agree with each asset's value?*
- *Do I agree with the inventory and amount of the debts?*

Go back to the financial statements that you and your spouse prepared and cross-reference the proposal against what is reported on the most recent financial statements.

Ask yourself:

- *Has anything been left off or unaccounted for?*
- *Are all the asset valuations current?*
- *Has there been an increase or decrease in debt?*

> ✔ **DO** go over the numbers with your attorney and your financial advisor. Speak up and ask questions about any detail you don't understand or any number that seems "off" to you.

DIG INTO THE DETAILS. Once you are comfortable that all assets, income, and debts have been accounted for and that all the values are accurate, it's time to unpack the details of the proposal. Be diligent and thorough. This is where the rubber meets the road.

Put the proposed share of your assets, liabilities, and income into a spreadsheet. Be sure to include proposed obligations to pay support, or the income you will receive from support. Take out the budget you prepared (see Chapter 5 for preparing a budget during your divorce).

Work with your financial advisor to project the potential value of all the assets you are being assigned, the liabilities you will need to cover, your expenses, and your total income from all sources, including what you will be paying or receiving in support. It is essential that you know what your income sources will be, what your debt obligations will be, what assets you will have, and how they will contribute to your income over time and your long-term financial security.

Ask yourself:

- *Do the numbers work?*

- *Do I have a plan for meeting my debt obligations? Do these numbers support that plan?*

- *Does the budget balance? Will my income cover my expenses?*

- *Is the budget sustainable? How much/how often will I need to draw on assets to cover my expenses?*

It is at this point you will realize where the proposal falls short and where it meets your needs. If it falls short, you can reduce your expenses by downsizing your spending, or upsize your income by getting a job, working more hours, or asking for a raise. Only through this analysis will the truth be exposed about whether the proposal is "good."

EVALUATE THE CONTINGENCY PLANS. Your settlement agreement is a forward-facing document. It's a plan for the future. To protect you and serve you well, it must account for future unexpected events and changes in your life. Before you sign an agreement, make sure you understand how your financial arrangements will change in the event of death, disability, changes to income for you or your spouse, job loss, relocation, remarriage, and failure to pay support.

Ask yourself:

- *What if I lose my job or my ex loses theirs? What happens then?*

- *What happens if there are unexpected expenses?*

- *What if I want to get married again?*

- *What happens if my ex gets married again?*

- *What happens if the kids want to live with my ex?*

- *What happens if my ex dies or becomes disabled?*

- *What happens if I die or become disabled?*

- *What if I get a second job—will I lose/pay more support?*

- *Is the final agreement modifiable?*

PREPARE YOUR COUNTERPROPOSAL. If there are elements in the proposal from your spouse that don't work, it's now your job to consider, What would make it work? Identify the gaps in the offer and fill them with your preferred solutions. If money can't solve the problem, what can the other side do to make it work? A different parenting schedule that allows you to work more? Selling the house and downsizing or renting? Create the deal that you want and review it with your attorney and financial advisor. Seek their input on identifying solutions to resolving financial gaps and other sticking points.

Questions to Ask Before You Reject a Settlement

You will repeat your cost-benefit analysis and settlement review for all your proposals and counterproposals until you reach an agreement that works. Before you turn down a settlement, ask yourself these questions:

- *Have I thought this through completely?*

- *Are my objections coming from a place of ego?*

- *Am I responding out of anger, frustration, jealousy, or revenge?*

- *Am I being reasonable?*

- *Am I looking at this logically?*

- *Do I truly understand the proposal?*

UNDERSTAND HOW THE AGREEMENT CAN BE MODI-FIED. Before you sign a final agreement, you need a clear and complete understanding of how the agreement may be modified in the future. State laws direct how, and under what circumstances, spousal and child support can be modified when one spouse's income increases or decreases or when a spouse remarries. Changing property settlement agreements is typically difficult, but there are circumstances where it is necessary and possible, especially when there is fraud or intentional misrepresentation. You may find it is necessary to correct an error in the agreement. Depending on state law, there may be specific circumstances and/or a limited window of time for you to take steps to modify a final property settlement if one spouse has lied or omitted information in their financial statements. It's essential that you know both state laws and the terms of your own agreement regarding modification so that you are prepared to act if you need to.

Chris's behavior changed drastically after temporary orders went into effect and his and Margo's case shifted to litigation. Chris tearfully admitted to spending money on a new romantic partner, and quickly returned some expensive jewelry and cancelled upcoming travel plans. Chris told Margo the affair was over. Chris begged Margo to give mediation another try, promising her full access to all their financial information and direct access to all financial accounts. Margo wasn't sure what the right call was. She worked through her cost-benefit analysis. Margo wanted the divorce to move forward, so she and her kids could reset their lives. She was really angry, often bitterly so, at Chris's actions, but her desire for resolution was what was driving her most, not a desire to punish. Litigation would come with a lot more legal fees. But in the end mediation would only be less expensive if it worked. And Margo didn't feel she could trust Chris in the process after his lying and stonewalling her about their finances. "I'll never know for sure what I don't know," she said to me. Margo also felt pretty certain that Chris's attitude and treatment of her could change again if they went back to mediation sessions. She didn't want to deal with him being disrespectful and dismissive of her, and who knows what else he might try to hide from her about their assets. She ultimately decided the safest route was to litigate. Margo would work with her attorney, Nancy, and Nancy would work with Chris's attorney, Brian, to negotiate the terms of their settlement.

The temporary support orders came in at the upper end of what Margo would likely have expected to receive in spousal support, and Nancy was able to negotiate a strong lump-sum figure for Margo in the final settlement agreement. Margo also received half of the funds Chris had spent on the affair. Margo and I worked very carefully together to document and project the kids' expenses, and Nancy negotiated a provision in the agreement that assigned specific responsibility to Chris for a majority share of those expenses, over and above the child support payments.

When their divorce decree was finally issued, Margo felt sorrowful, but her overwhelming emotion was relief. She also felt proud of herself for (mostly) keeping her cool and making thoughtful, rational decisions to keep her divorce on track, under some very intense emotional circumstances. Chris, she told me, was still complaining about the lawyer fees. Had Chris run a cost-benefit analysis on their actions at the start of their divorce, he'd have realized what a losing proposition it was to try to hide assets. Had Chris played things straight and fair from the start, their divorce might well have moved more quickly and less expensively through mediation—and the final numbers might have been slightly better for Chris than they turned out to be. But none of that was Margo's problem anymore.

Key Takeaways and Next Steps

- Rational, future-oriented decision-making is essential to navigating your divorce successfully. Maintaining perspective can be hard to do when your emotions are running high.

- A holistic cost-benefit analysis takes into account the financial and emotional stakes of your decisions, and can help you stay focused on your most important priorities and goals. This decision-making framework can be applied to nearly every decision you make in your divorce and can save you time, money, emotional stress, and energy throughout the process.

- A holistic cost-benefit analysis is an invaluable tool for when it comes time to consider settlement proposals. When evaluating a proposed settlement: Take your time. Make sure you understand every word. Double-check the numbers for accuracy, making sure all assets and debts are included and values are correct. Carefully review contingency plans. Run the proposed numbers with your financial advisor to determine whether what's being offered is sustainable for you over the long term.

PART THREE

AFTER THE DIVORCE

CHAPTER EIGHT

Tackling Your Post-Divorce To-Do List

The legal end of a marriage comes with a tremendous range and complexity of emotions. Your day in court is bittersweet. Whether you consider it the end of an era, the end of a nightmare, or the end of a dream, your life has changed. So much of your daily thoughts and activities have been caught up in working on your divorce; you've now entered a new transitional stage of the process. Some of your core team of professionals—your attorney, paralegals, some of the people in your support system who have shared the journey with you—will slowly bow out of your daily life, and your new reality will begin to take shape.

Challenging as it may have been at times, treating your divorce like a business transaction can, in the end, make the critical difference between leaving the courthouse feeling terrified and overwhelmed, still battered by the storm, and feeling free to chart your future as captain of your own ship, even as you continue to grieve and process the end of your marriage.

And you need to stick with that business mindset, because there is important work to do after your divorce is final. Divorce leaves a lot of loose ends, and now is the time to tie them up securely so you can move on with your life.

Get Organized

There's a lot of follow-up to be done on the matters that you just spent months or years negotiating. The first six months after a divorce is a busy time, with a lot of detail-oriented, time-sensitive, financially consequential tasks to complete. You've got assets to separate, property deeds and titles to transfer, new insurance to apply for, beneficiaries to update, financial accounts to close and open, and more. Most of your tasks will come with a due date or deadline, and you can lose out on money, incur additional taxes, and face legal trouble if you don't comply. Getting your post-divorce work done right, and on schedule, matters—and things will inevitably fall through the cracks if you don't write it all down and keep track of your progress.

If your attorney is good, they will provide you with a checklist and timeline of the matters you need to address. If your attorney didn't provide you with an aftercare checklist, your first step will be to create one yourself. Before you do anything else, set up an online calendar, make a new spreadsheet, or dedicate a notebook to mapping out and tracking your tasks for the next several months. You don't want to forget to close a bank account or to make a money transfer on time.

Make no mistake: there can be major financial consequences for not being attentive to every detail of your agreement. I had a client whose spouse forgot when he was supposed to stop paying spousal support and continued to pay for years beyond when his obligation legally ended. He didn't schedule the end date for his automatic monthly payments, filed away his divorce degree, and forgot about it. I had another client who forgot that she was due funds from a trust after a certain number of years. She was more than pleasantly surprised when I informed her the money was coming, because I had it on my calendar.

> ✔ **DO** request multiple copies of your divorce agreement. It's a good idea to have at least two fully executed copies of your agreement, as well as a copy of your divorce decree signed by the judge. Your attorney can help you get these copies, or you can request them yourself from the court clerk. Store your divorce documents securely, with your birth certificate, will, powers of attorney, medical directives, and other important documents.

Read and Mark Up Your Divorce Decree

People run into trouble when they don't understand the next steps after a divorce. Your divorce decree is your road map for the tasks and obligations that need your attention. Read it carefully, line by line. Transfer all your action items with corresponding due dates and other details to your calendar or spreadsheet. Pay particular attention to those deadlines. Your agreement may state that you have a certain period to pay a debt transfer property to your spouse. And if you are paying child or spousal support, there will be a start date for those financial obligations to begin. For every action item on your calendar or list, make sure you know the *what*, the *when*, and the *how*: *what* you need to accomplish, *when* it must be done, and *how* this task is to be completed successfully. Pay close attention to details of your agreement about child-related matters, such as providing notice to your ex about your children's schedule, activities, or other information. If there are any details in your decree that you don't understand clearly, ask your lawyer to explain and clarify. And follow the directions of your agreement to the letter. You don't have to like everything you're obligated to do as a result of your divorce—nobody does—but you must comply. If you don't, legal and financial trouble may await you.

★ *Gabrielle's Pro Tip* Don't wait to ask your attorney to prepare deed transfers, car transfers, or other legal documents needed to transfer property. Agreements typically state that transfers must be executed within thirty days of the date a divorce is final. At this point, lawyer fatigue has probably set in, and the last thing you want to face is more legal fees. But if anything happens to the property, the insurance company will make the check payable to you and your spouse, which could pose a problem.

Transfer Property

You may be required to transfer property to your ex, or you may be expecting a property transfer to you. The work you'll need to do depends on the type of property involved.

REAL ESTATE. If you or your spouse is keeping the marital home or another real estate property, the deed will need to be transferred. Have your attorney prepare a deed transfer. These transfers will need the notarized signature of the spouse departing the deed and will need to be filed with the property records office in the county where the property resides. If you and your ex did a buyout of your home or other property as part of your divorce, the deed may already have been transferred if the mortgage was refinanced. If you're not sure, check with your lawyer.

🔥 *Red Flag* Transferring a deed and removing an ex-spouse from a mortgage are two separate steps. You can be off a property deed and remain on a mortgage and be liable for the debt if your ex fails to pay. If you are leaving the ownership of a property that your ex-spouse will continue to own, make sure the deed has been transferred and you've taken action to remove yourself from any existing mortgage.

VEHICLES. Cars, motorcycles, RVs, and boats that one spouse is keeping will need titles transferred to their name. If you are the spouse giving up ownership, you will need to take care of the title transfer. Typically, title transfers for vehicles are done through your state's Department of Motor Vehicles. If there is a loan against a car or other vehicle, make sure your spouse has refinanced and you have been removed from the loan, so you're not liable if your ex doesn't pay the loan or makes late payments, which can hurt your credit.

✔ **DO** open a checking account in your name if you haven't already.

CASH AND INVESTMENTS. Close your remaining joint checking and savings accounts and have each spouse's share of the balance transferred to new accounts or have the bank draft checks to be mailed to each of you. If you divided investment assets in-kind, you will need to open a new account to receive your share of the stocks or other investment funds. If you agreed to sell and split the proceeds, you should have agreed to a date for the sale. If the sale hasn't yet taken place, make sure it takes place as scheduled, and that you receive your share of the proceeds.

> ✔ **DO** put all your requests to close accounts and transfer funds in writing to your financial institutions.

OTHER PROPERTY. Work out an arrangement with your ex to give them, or obtain for yourself, the personal property that you are each keeping. Don't let your ex's belongings linger in your spare bedroom or anywhere in your space, and don't delay in retrieving your property from your ex's home. A clean break and a fresh start will serve everyone's best interests.

Follow Up on QDRO and Other Retirement Transfers

If you are to receive funds from your ex's qualified retirement plans, follow up with your lawyer to confirm that all QDROs have been submitted. If you are to receive funds from your ex-spouse's IRA as part of your settlement, you will need to establish an IRA for that transfer. If your IRA is being split and funds transferred to your ex, you will need to request that transfer in accordance with the deadline in your divorce decree.

★ *Gabrielle's Pro Tip* Remember, IRA-IRA transfers are nontaxable events. So are QDRO transfers. If you then take retirement funds and deposit them into a nonretirement account, you will need to pay taxes on those funds as income, and you will owe an early withdrawal penalty if you are younger than 59½. The IRS early withdrawal penalty is 10 percent of the amount distributed and reported on your tax return. Work with your financial advisor to make sure retirement asset transfers are executed to avoid tax liability and early withdrawal penalties. If you need access to these retirement assets now to fund your new life—to pay off debts or put toward a down payment on a new home, for example—consult with your financial advisor and CPA before you decide to sell or transfer funds, and make sure your financial plan includes paying all taxes and penalties associated with the transfer.

Close Your Joint Credit Card Accounts

If you have any remaining credit card accounts with your ex, now is the time to close them. Put your requests to financial institutions in writing. If your divorce decree makes your ex-spouse responsible for paying off marital credit card debt in the future, you remain liable for that debt if your spouse doesn't pay. You can contact the financial institution, in writing, and request that you be removed from the account. (Include a copy of your divorce decree to show the company that it is your ex's responsibility to pay the debt.) The credit card company may not agree to take you off the account, and you can still be held legally liable for the unpaid debt even if they do remove you. But you will have established a record with the company that may be helpful if you need to go to court over these unpaid debts in the future.

Change Your Beneficiaries

Everything on your post-divorce to-do list is important and timely. This step is one you'll want to do immediately. Your now ex-spouse may be the beneficiary on your life insurance; your IRA, 401(k), pension, or annuity; investment accounts with pay- or transfer-on-death designations; or any other asset that names a beneficiary in the event of your death. Contact each company for instructions about updating your beneficiaries. If you forget to do this and you pass away, chances are your ex will likely get the proceeds. If this happens, your ex can choose to disclaim the benefit and give it to any successor beneficiaries who are listed.

> ✖ **DON'T** delay changing your beneficiaries because you're not yet certain about how you want to distribute your assets in an estate plan. You can easily change your beneficiaries again down the road. I talk more about beneficiary designation and estate planning in Chapter 9.

Change Your Will and Powers of Attorney

You'll also want to immediately remove your ex-spouse as an inheritor of your property and designate new heirs to receive assets from your estate in the event of your death. And if your ex-spouse remains designated as your power of attorney, you need to change this right away. Otherwise, your ex will have the legal right to make decisions about your money if you are unable to.

> ✔ **DO** remove your spouse as your health care proxy—the person who makes your medical decisions if you are incapacitated—if you didn't take this step at the outset of your divorce.

Set Up Your New Health Insurance

Your health insurance may be changing as a result of your divorce. Your divorce agreement may obligate your ex to pay for your health insurance, or you may be taking on the financial responsibility yourself. In either case, you need to make sure you have your new coverage in place before your old coverage ends. (If you haven't yet decided what health insurance coverage is right for you in the first stage of your post-divorce life, review your insurance options in Chapter 5.) If you're planning to take COBRA coverage through your ex-spouse's employer, you will have a limited time in which to notify the plan administrator that you intend to do so. Remember, unless it's addressed otherwise in your agreement, you will be responsible for paying the monthly COBRA premiums. Divorce is considered a qualifying event by the ACA, so you can purchase health insurance through a state marketplace or the federal website (*www.healthcare.gov*) at any point during the year, outside of the annual enrollment period.

Follow Through on Your Name Change

If you asked the judge to approve a name change in your divorce, you need to update your accounts and important documents with your new name. Notify all relevant agencies, financial institutions, and companies and follow their directions:

- IRS (and be sure to file your taxes under your new name)
- Social Security Administration (you will be issued a new card)
- Your state's Department of Motor Vehicles (you will need a new driver's license and registration issued)
- US Postal Service
- Your county Registrar of Voters
- US Department of State, for an updated passport (*www.travel.state .gov/passport*)
- Your employer (you may need to work with human resources or directly with the companies that provide employee benefits)
- Insurance companies: mortgage, auto, life, disability, and any other insurance you hold
- Credit card companies
- Banks where you have checking, savings, and money market accounts
- Financial institutions where you have mortgages, car loans, and other loans
- Financial institutions where you have brokerage accounts
- Companies that provide you services and issue you bills, including utilities, cell phone, subscriptions, and memberships

> ✔ **DO** be consistent in applying your new name to all the documents and financial accounts in your life.

Be Diligent About Recordkeeping

Develop a recordkeeping system that works best for you and stick with it routinely from here on out. Online accounting software like Quicken is a great tool for tracking and managing your financial data. Use Dropbox to store and organize online receipts and important documents. You and your ex can consider using a shared Dropbox folder to share information and documentation about your children, including school report cards and medical records; just make sure your personal records are stored in a folder that your ex does not have permission to access. Keep track of receipts and invoices related to all your shared expenses. This will make your periodic settling up with your ex over shared expenses easier and less prone to discord. And you'll have the documentation you need should you have to get the court involved. If you must prove that you paid something and don't have any records, you may not get reimbursed.

> ✔ **DON'T** let go of your emotional support team. Keep working with your therapist and continue to rely on the relationships and resources of your support group for as long as you need to. The emotional fallout of divorce doesn't end just because you've reached your legal destination.

Update Your Team

You'll want to get help from an updated team of professionals to help you make the full transition to your new life in good financial standing.

Find an estate planning attorney and meet with them as soon as possible to draft new documents. You need a new will, health care proxy,

power of attorney, trust, living will, and Do Not Resuscitate (DNR) directive, and there are a lot of important financial and legal considerations
that go into making these arrangements after you've divorced. You can
ask your divorce attorney, CPA, or financial advisor to refer you to someone they trust.

When choosing an estate planning attorney, seek an experienced
lawyer who will take the time to understand your wishes, aspirations,
and desires before drafting the documents. Emotions run high after a
divorce; there may be tension in your family and with your children, and
you may feel conflicted when thinking about how you want your assets
handled after your death. You want to work with an estate planning
attorney who understands both the financial and interpersonal com-
plications associated with planning after divorce. Be sure to ask them if
they have the time to put toward not only drafting your documents but
also educating you about your estate planning options. Ask them how
much they charge, how many hours they expect to spend on the drafting, if they charge for changes and addendums, and if they offer a flat fee.

Similarly, you'll want to work with **a CPA with experience in tax
analysis and tax preparation for people who have recently divorced**.
If you're working with the same CPA you used during your marriage and
your ex is still working with them, too, consider finding a new accountant for a fresh start. You can ask your financial advisor and your estate
planning attorney for recommendations for a CPA with the right experience to meet your needs.

A **financial advisor** will work with you to develop a comprehensive
long-term financial plan, help you make decisions about how to invest
and manage the assets you received in your divorce, help you plan for
your retirement, and advise you on financial matters in your estate
plan. If you've been working with a financial advisor who specializes in
divorce, you may decide to continue working with them. You may decide
to return to a financial advisor you worked with before your divorce or
find a new advisor. However you proceed, make sure you're working with
a registered investment advisor who is qualified to give you strategic
advice on your investment options. Be sure your financial advisor is a
fiduciary—a financial professional who is legally and ethically obligated

to advise you and act in your best interests. Certified divorce financial planners (CDFAs), certified financial planners (CFPs), and registered investment advisors (RIAs) all have fiduciary responsibility; they are legally bound to put your interests ahead of their own. You can check their credentials through the Institute for Divorce Financial Analysts (*www.institutedfa.com.*), the Certified Financial Planner Board of Standards (*www.cfp.net*), and the Financial Industry Regulatory Authority (*www.brokercheck.com*).

Be sure you understand up front how they charge for their services. (See Chapter 1 for a review of how financial advisors structure their fees.)

QUESTIONS FOR YOUR FINANCIAL ADVISOR

- *Which accounts are being transferred?*
- *Do I have to sell positions? Will there be a tax consequence?*
- *Do I need to make tax payments?*
- *Can the mortgage be paid from my account automatically?*
- *Is the life insurance in place to protect my support payments?*
- *Has all of my money been transferred?*

Key Takeaways and Next Steps

- Take a breath, relax, and recover from all your hard work. Give yourself time and get support to process the emotions that come up for you as your divorce ends. Recharge emotionally and physically, and focus on acclimating to your new life, a life without divorce at its center.

- Make sure you understand every single task and deadline that you're responsible for in your divorce agreement. Ask questions of your attorney and financial advisor until you are crystal clear on your entire to-do list. All the details matter—be vigilant and thorough.

- Use a calendar or spreadsheet to keep track of every one of your post-divorce tasks and their deadlines. Keep it up to date.

- Immediately change your beneficiaries to your will, life insurance, and other assets that have transfer-on-death arrangements. Change your power of attorney and health care proxy.

- Update your team with an estate planning attorney, and line up financial professionals to help you develop a long-term financial plan that includes retirement.

CHAPTER NINE

Your Future Belongs to You

Putting Your Plans into Action

The future you've been waiting to embrace is here. To make good on all the promise it holds, you need to take stock of where you are now, financially and emotionally, and where you want to go. Your money is yours to manage on your own. Now is the time to develop a long-term financial plan and to plan for your retirement and your estate. In this new chapter of your financial life you will benefit from—and build on—what you learned and achieved in working through the process of your divorce. You'll be working with new numbers and a different set of financial considerations. You'll also have full control and autonomy over your decisions, and the hard-earned confidence that comes from the experience you've gained.

Rest and Reflect on Your Journey

You've been through a difficult, demanding, complex, emotionally grueling experience, one that has tested you and likely transformed you in ways you're just beginning to recognize. Carve out time to rest, to reconnect with a life that isn't dominated by the work of your divorce. Spend time with friends and family who enrich your life. Prioritize fun, relaxation, and sleep. And as you're decompressing and finding new equilibrium and routine in your life, spend some quiet, reflective time thinking about how your divorce has changed you. Ask yourself:

- *What have learned?*
- *What do I want in my life?*
- *Who do I want to be?*
- *What makes me happy?*
- *What scares me, what makes me sad, what makes me feel confident?*
- *Where do I want to be in the next year, or two years, or three?*
- *What do I want my lifestyle to look like and feel like?*

Remove any pressure to arrive quickly at answers, or for those answers to arrive neatly tied up in a bow. Divorce ushered great change into your life, and you may feel the impact of those changes in waves for some time. As you recover from your divorce and move forward with your life, allow yourself the time and mental and emotional space to explore how you're feeling and what you want. Your divorce has earned you a freedom of choice you haven't had in a long time, maybe ever. *What do you want to do with it?*

Establish a New Financial Status Quo

Your finances need time to settle out, too. You've gone through your budget time and time again. Now it's showtime, and the numbers are real. Be extra cautious, attentive, and thoughtful about your spending in the first year after your divorce. Fresh off a divorce, people frequently make snap decisions or overextend themselves. This often translates to living beyond their means, and regret and stress down the road. You may have a lump sum that makes you feel flush with cash. (That lump sum needs to support you over time.) You may feel a financial and emotional freedom that you haven't had in years. (You protect your emotional and financial freedom by planning and spending within your means.) Guard against emotional spending and financial decision-making, just as you did in your divorce. Make sure you understand your numbers and take time to observe your cash flow in your new life. Ease yourself into your new, independent financial life: do your best to avoid making any significant financial decisions or commitments within the first twelve months of your divorce. If you feel you need to make a major financial move, consult with your financial advisor before you act. Otherwise, let things settle, clear your head, meet with your CPA and estate planning attorney, and work with your financial advisor on a long-term financial plan.

> ✖ **DON'T** make *any* major decisions, including moving in with a new partner, for the first year. Spend time recovering from the divorce process and take time for yourself. This experience has likely changed you in ways you may not yet realize. Give yourself ample time to get acquainted with the "new" you.

UPDATE YOUR NET WORTH AND CASH FLOW STATEMENTS

Your mix of assets, debt, income, and expenses is different than what it was when you were married and when you were going through your divorce. To make sound choices that will serve you well over the long term, you need to stay plugged in to what you have, earn, owe, and spend. This is the foundation of your routine financial management and the figures you'll use to develop a long-term plan. Continue to retain all your statements and update your account balances regularly in Quicken or your financial spreadsheet.

> ✔ **DON'T** ignore your financial statements! Open them promptly and file them in your Dropbox folder or whatever system you're using to organize your financial documents. Transfer current values to Quicken or whatever management tool you're using to track your finances.

CREATE AN EMERGENCY FUND

Keep at least six months of funds for your living expenses available in your local bank account in case of an emergency. If you need time to build this emergency reserve, make this your first priority for saving. Without an emergency fund, you will have to dip into your other assets—or borrow and rack up debt—to meet unanticipated expenses or sudden changes in income. That pressure can force you to make snap financial decisions that don't serve your long-term interests. (And if you have illiquid stocks or investments that need to be sold to raise the cash that you need, it could take up to three days to receive the funds.) Build a safety net.

How to Handle a Lump-Sum Payment

You just received a large sum of money. This doesn't mean that you're rich. If you received these funds as an alimony buyout, you opted for a lump sum over periodic payments. You're not going to be getting monthly support payments. Instead, you must make these funds last for as long as possible. Consult with your financial advisor to learn how to properly and responsibly manage your funds so that they can sustain you for years to come.

UNDERSTAND YOUR NEW TAX REALITY

Going from married to unmarried changes your tax position. You'll be filing your taxes differently, as either single or head of household. Your income, deductions, and credits have changed. You're working with a different mix of assets you may be wondering about selling or investing for retirement. Don't wait until tax season to meet with your CPA and get up to speed on the changes that are coming, and the tax implications of any major financial decisions you're considering for next year. (Remember, ideally, you're going to wait a full year before making any big financial moves.)

> ✔ **DO** always consider the tax consequences of your financial decisions and seek guidance and clarification from your CPA or financial advisor *before* you act.

Over the long term, divorce can bring tax benefits and tax obligations that can easily fall under the radar without professional guidance. For example, if you're required by your financial settlement to fund your children's education, you need to be aware of potential gift tax implications. Although your direct tuition payments (even for adult children) are exempt from gift tax when these payments are a requirement in your divorce agreement, your payments for related educational expenses (such as books and room and board) may be subject to gift tax. Let's say you're paying $20,000 in tuition directly to your child's university and giving your college student $15,000 in cash for living expenses. The tuition won't be a taxable gift, but the cash may be.

> ✖ **DON'T** sell assets without first speaking with your financial advisor or CPA to understand the tax implications of any sale you're considering.

Long-Term Financial Planning After Your Divorce

Long-term financial planning and planning for retirement change when you go through a divorce. Your financial picture has changed. Your goals and expectations for the *what, where, why, when,* and *how* of your retirement have likely changed, too, whether by necessity, desire, or both. Your interests for your life in your next chapter may be changing, too, now that you are in the driver's seat, in full control of your choices, with the freedom to plan for a retirement lifestyle that suits you. Your passions and your priorities are the only ones that matter. To make good on them, you need to plan carefully and give yourself the benefit of time to cultivate the financial resources you'll need to fund your goals.

Divorce adds layers of complexity to long-term financial planning. You're working with a different income stream and a different roster of expenses, a new mix of assets, and debts that are your sole responsibility. You may have a lump-sum settlement to manage. Your tax status has changed, and the financial settlement of your divorce may have you considering whether to sell assets, which comes with tax implications. Once again, you're working to create a puzzle from a lot of moving pieces that you'll need to move around, trying out different combinations to see what works best.

> ✔ **DO** work with a financial advisor to strategize the best use of your assets to produce income to replace your spousal support when it ends.

ORGANIZE YOUR FINANCIAL INFORMATION

To plan effectively for your long-term financial future, you need to know your numbers. As a first step, make sure you have current statements and documents for all your assets, debts, income, and expenses. If you've been keeping your records up to date and managing your financial information in Quicken or in a spreadsheet, you should be ready to go. Give it all a careful review.

> ✔ **DO** imagine your ideal day (or week, or month) in retirement. What's the pace of life like? Where are you? Who are you seeing? How are you engaging your mind? Your body?

START CREATING YOUR LONG-TERM VISION

It's time to dive back into envisioning the future you want. This time, you can think specifically of your retirement years: how you want to spend your time; where you'd like to live; what interests, relationships, and causes you want to prioritize. Break out the tools from your initial vision work to create a rich, textured, vivid picture of your life in your retirement years: build a vision board, do a brain dump, start a conversation with your future self. (See Chapter 3 if you need a refresh on tools to help you craft a vision for the future.)

ASK YOURSELF:

- *Do I want to work in retirement? Part-time? Full-time? Not at all?*

- *Is there a new business venture or passion project I want to devote myself to?*

- *Do I want to spend time volunteering, helping others? What are the causes, issues, or communities I'd like to support with my time?*

- *How active do I want to be? When I think about my ideal day, week, or month, do I imagine lots of quiet days, a busy calendar, or something in between?*

- *Who are the family and friends I want to spend time with?*

- *How important is it to me to be near old friends or current friends?*

- *How do I feel about making new friends, and developing a new network and community in retirement?*

- *What do I want my community to look like, feel like?*

- *Where do I want to live?*

- *Is my current home suitable for aging in place?*

- *Do I want to travel?*

- *How often? For how long?*

- *What are the places I'd like to visit?*

- *How do I feel about traveling alone?*

- *Does my vision of retirement include funding major purchases? Renovating a home or buying a vacation property? Paying for a wedding? Funding education for children or grandchildren?*

- *Are there people in my family I anticipate wanting or needing to care for or support while I'm in retirement?*

- *What kinds of support do I want to provide with my time and/or my money?*

START PRIORITIZING

After you develop some raw material to work with, spend some time thinking about what elements of your vision are more, and less, important to you. Make a list of your retirement goals and rank them from most to least important. Or rate each one on an importance scale from 1 to 10. This will help you identify what you need most. When you start making decisions about how to save, invest, and direct funds for retirement, you can focus first on your top priorities and then work to achieve your other hopes and dreams.

EXAMINE YOUR FEARS

As when you created a vision for your future after divorce, your retirement vision should include a thoughtful examination of your fears. Understanding your fears can point you to vulnerabilities in your financial plan, make you more attentive to addressing health concerns, and bring to the surface emotional wounds and worries that you can address with your therapist. We all have fears about the future and about growing older. When you know what yours are, you can work intentionally to address them and make your life today—and your future life—more peaceful and financially secure.

Most people carry some combination of long-term worries about their money, health, and relationships. As you imagine your future retirement, pay attention to the concerns and fears that keep coming up.

ASK YOURSELF:

What are my financial concerns? Common financial concerns about retirement include:

- Not being able to support yourself without working

- Not having enough income from sources other than employment earnings

- Losing money in the stock market or having other investments go down in value

- Overspending in retirement

- Being cash poor, with funds tied up in a house or other illiquid assets

- Not having enough funds to last for your lifetime

- Not having an estate to leave heirs

- Heirs incurring estate taxes

What are my health concerns? Common health concerns include:

- How current health issues will impact retirement

- Family health history

- Needing—and affording—nursing home care, assisted living, or home health care

- Dying young

- Living too long

What are my family and relationship concerns? Common relationship concerns include:

- Not seeing family enough—being lonely or bored in retirement

- Seeing too much of family—not having enough privacy, freedom, space, and independence

- Parents needing financial/emotional/direct support and care during your retirement years

- Children needing financial/emotional/direct support and care during your retirement years

- Children wanting or needing to live with you

- Children not being able to manage money responsibly

DECIDE WHEN YOU WANT TO RETIRE

Your answer will affect how you create a long-term financial plan that secures your financial life throughout retirement. Your target age for retirement, together with your current age, will establish the time frame you have to fund your retirement goals. It's important to identify your desired retirement age. Next, think about how willing you are to push back that retirement date, if it meant you could fund a larger share of your goals. Delaying retirement may be necessary to give you the time to build the financial security you need. You may decide to push back retirement so you can fund more of the lifestyle that appeals to you. There are no wrong answers here. It's valuable to understand clearly what you are willing to trade to have the experiences and lifestyle you want. If the numbers don't work to meet your goals on your ideal timetable, how will you adjust? Plan for a later retirement? Work part-time? Scale back or change some of your goals?

The legwork I've described will help you develop a picture of your long-term future and the retirement life you want to achieve: the *what*, *where*, *when*, and *why*. Your next step is to think about the *how*. How will you make a version of this future a reality? How will you fund the retirement chapter of your life? To answer these questions, it's time, once again, to dig deeply into your numbers. I strongly recommend working with a financial advisor to develop a comprehensive, long-term financial plan that includes retirement. I am going to share some guidance for examining and projecting your income and expenses over the long term. But there is no substitute for the hands-on expertise and support of a qualified, experienced financial advisor in creating a solid, sustainable, secure financial plan for your long-term future.

ANTICIPATE YOUR EXPENSES

To establish a realistic and sustainable long-term financial plan that supports you through retirement, you need to think well ahead about your expenses, both your essential living expenses—what it will cost to pay your bills throughout your life—and major expenses you expect to take on or encounter.

START WITH YOUR CURRENT BUDGET. Stay closely connected to your budget. Keep your numbers current and track your spending carefully. That's how you develop a clear understanding of what you need to meet your basic needs in the current chapter of your life. And your understanding of your current expenses becomes a template for you to adjust as you plan for life's future chapters.

EXPECT THE UNEXPECTED. Your emergency fund isn't an "extra" or a luxury. It's an essential component of your short- and long-term financial security. It provides you with the resources you need when things go suddenly sideways—you lose your job, your house needs major repairs, your car conks out and you must buy a new one, today. When you draw from your emergency fund, make it a priority to replenish the funds as quickly as you can. Use your emergency fund for real financial emergencies, not for trips or spending sprees or other wants. When you have an emergency fund to draw on, you are less likely to need to have to quickly sell or draw on other assets or accrue significant debt to pay for the unexpected. And that keeps your long-term financial planning on track.

RECOGNIZE THAT YOUR EXPENSES WILL CHANGE OVER TIME. As you look ahead to the long term and your retirement, identify expenses that may change over time. Some expenses may decrease or go away altogether—you may pay off a mortgage or down-size your home and spend less to maintain it, and your children will become financially independent. Other expenses may increase. Anticipating long-term changes to your expenses enables you to develop a realistic picture of your future needs, and the income you'll require to meet them.

> ✔ **DO** plan for long-term care expenses as you age and consider applying for long-term care insurance if you can afford it. I talk more about long-term care insurance later in this chapter.

✔ **DO** plan to enroll in Medicare insurance when you turn sixty-five, even if you anticipate receiving retiree health benefits from your employer. Most retiree health care benefit plans require you to enroll in Medicare to cover basic medical costs. And employers can make changes to retiree benefits, leaving you without the level of coverage you anticipated.

✔ **DO** consider Medigap insurance as a future expense, and budget for the monthly premium. These are supplemental plans issued by insurance companies that help pay expenses that Medicare doesn't cover and may be used to help cover Medicare copayments and deductibles.

BUDGET AND SAVE FOR BIG-TICKET ITEMS. Want to contribute to your children's college education? Expect to pay for a child's wedding one day? Want a new car every three or four years? Interested in taking a long vacation or major trip once a year? Whatever big-ticket events or experiences are on your horizon, plan for how you'll pay for them. When you make these major expenses a part of your financial plan, they are far less likely to disrupt that plan—and you keep your finances on track for the long term.

LOOK FOR WAYS TO REDUCE YOUR EXPENSES. Most of us are spending money on things we don't need, don't use, or don't value as a spending priority. Be routinely on the lookout for ways to lower your expenses, to make room in your current cash flow and preserve your funds over the long term. Don't disregard any expense as too small to matter. Every dollar counts. Do you need all those streaming services, sports channels, subscriptions? Get in the habit of periodically reviewing your regular expenses to see what you might eliminate.

✔ **DO** spend within your means. You don't know how long you will live, so plan accordingly.

ANTICIPATE YOUR INCOME

Where is the money coming from to pay your bills, meet your basic needs, and cover the "extras"—the wishes and wants you have for your future life and your retirement years? No matter how far in the future you think retirement may be, now is the time to think ahead about the sources of income you'll draw on to fund your lifestyle. Divorce has changed your current and future income stream. Beyond what you negotiated in your divorce, your spouse's retirement income is no longer available to you. It's critical that you plan well ahead and make informed choices to ensure you have the resources you need to support yourself throughout the rest of your life.

- *If you are employed, are you contributing to your employer's retirement plans?*
- *Have you established an IRA to save for retirement on your own?*
- *Do you know how assets you received in your divorce will produce income for you over the long term?*
- *Are there assets you expect to sell to generate retirement funds?*
- *Will you work part-time in retirement? For how long?*
- *Do you anticipate an inheritance?*
- *Can you start saving more to fund your future? How much more per month could you save rather than spend?*

What Will You Do When Your Spousal Support Ends?

If you are receiving spousal support, you must plan ahead for the day when that support ends. Don't wait until your support is almost finished to develop a strategy to replace the income that you will lose. If you will be sixty-two or older at the time your support ends, you have the option to take your Social Security benefit. But before you do, be careful to review your spousal Social Security benefit, if you are eligible for it. Compare the values to see if you'll have more income taking half of your ex-spouse's share (at full retirement age) than what you will receive if you take all of your own benefit. Be sure to create an account at *www.ssa.gov* to review your benefits and your ex-spouse's benefits. (Remember, you'll need your ex's Social Security number to review their benefits.) And start planning now for the future change in your income that will happen when your support ceases.

Don't ignore the fact that your support will be ending. Don't bury your head in the sand and expect to get an extension. Under certain circumstances, it's possible to qualify for an extension of spousal support, but these extensions are difficult to obtain. Discuss this with your attorney.

CONSIDER YOUR INSURANCE COVERAGE OPTIONS

Deciding what insurance you need is a critical element of long-term financial planning after a divorce. The right insurance provides financial protection for you and your children through the next chapters of your life. And it can help you preserve your assets to pass along after your death. Talk with your financial advisor and your estate planning attorney about how these insurance options fit into your long-term financial plan.

Life insurance enables you to provide money to beneficiaries after your death. There are several types of life insurance. The two main types are *term life insurance*, which provides coverage over a defined period of time, and *permanent life insurance*, which lasts for as long as you keep it in place by paying the premium. Permanent life insurance has a cash value; you can borrow against your life insurance benefit during your lifetime. Some life insurance policies also have provisions that allow you to use some of your benefit while you are alive—for example, if you have a terminal illness and need to pay for care. You will need to share some health information and may need a medical exam to qualify for life insurance, and for the insurance company to set your premium costs.

✔ **DO** meet with an insurance professional to determine how to best manage your life insurance policies. Consider having a trust be the beneficiary of your life insurance. (See more below about trusts in estate planning.) Ask your financial advisor or CPA to recommend an insurance professional they trust.

Disability insurance will provide you with a portion of your income if you become unable to work because of injury or illness. You may have access to disability insurance through your employer, or you can purchase disability insurance yourself. The cost of disability insurance will be affected by how long a disability period the coverage provides for, how much income it covers, how long you must hold the policy before you are eligible to receive benefits, and how generous the policy is in defining a threshold for disability and allowing access to benefits.

★ *Gabrielle's Pro Tip*   If you don't have dependents, you don't need life insurance. Do consider long-term care insurance if you can afford it.

Long-term care insurance can be a help in paying for costs if you eventually are unable to take care of yourself without assistance. It may provide funds for home health care, residential care in assisted living facilities, or other support to meet your daily needs. Having long-term care insurance in place can provide you with funds to access the level of care you want and need as you age. And it can help you protect assets you want to leave to your heirs from being drained by extended and expensive care costs. You should expect that a medical exam and review of your medical history will be required to purchase a policy. Long-term care insurance can be difficult to qualify for, depending on your age and any health issues in your history. And this insurance gets harder to obtain—and more expensive—the older you are when you apply. If you're interested in long-term care insurance, don't wait to get the ball rolling.

Estate Planning

Everyone needs a written estate plan. Without one, state law will determine where your assets go. Your estate plan lets you direct how you want your assets distributed after your death. It ensures that financial and medical decisions are made in accordance with your wishes if you become incapacitated. How you structure your estate plan will depend on your goals and the financial composition of your estate. Comprehensive estate planning can help you:

- Minimize estate taxes
- Use assets to fund your retirement and also preserve an estate to pass along to heirs
- Make sure your heirs receive the assets you want them to inherit
- Ensure that decisions about your assets are made in line with your intentions if you become incapacitated
- Transfer ownership of assets to beneficiaries before your death
- Direct how and when beneficiaries will use and benefit from assets you designate to them
- Minimize conflict among your heirs

UPDATE YOUR WILL. Think about the people and causes you want to support with your money. Think also about the items you would like to give to your individual heirs. Meet with your heirs ahead of time to discuss your intentions and share the thinking that led to your decisions. Be open with your children or other heirs now, to avoid hurt feelings after your death.

UPDATE OR ESTABLISH A POWER OF ATTORNEY. This is the person you authorize to make decisions about your assets in the event that you are unable to make these decisions yourself. Your power of attorney acts as your agent and your proxy in financial matters. Choose with care someone you trust and who has demonstrated responsible decision-making around property and finances.

CREATE A LIVING WILL. A living will is a legal document that articulates your wishes for receiving, or withholding, certain medical treatments if you are unable to communicate these wishes yourself. Intended to address the most serious and life-threatening medical circumstances, a living will clarifies your wishes about what treatments and interventions you want doctors to use to keep you alive, and any measures you do not want taken, with the understanding

that withholding measures may lead to your death. These are difficult circumstances to think about. Your estate planning attorney can
provide you with information and guidance about developing a living
will that expresses your wishes clearly and specifically. It will be up
to you to decide what directions to include. You can say what care you
want provided and what care you do not want. You can include your
wishes about decisions such as organ donation, end-of-life interventions to prolong your life, palliative treatment to relieve pain, and
religious or spiritual considerations you want applied to your care.
Your living will should include a DNR directive, a provision that specifically informs doctors whether you want them to resuscitate you if
you stop breathing or your heart stops beating.

> ✔ **DO** create a DNR directive even if you choose not to create a living will.
> While a DNR can be included in a living will, these are separate documents,
> and creating a DNR directive (a medical document) does not require a living
> will (a legal document). Your estate planning attorney can help you create
> both documents.

UPDATE OR ESTABLISH A HEALTH CARE PROXY. Your health
care proxy, sometimes referred to as a medical power of attorney, is
a person you designate to make health care decisions if you cannot
make them yourself. Your health care proxy will make decisions
based on the directions you have outlined in your living will.

CONSIDER ESTABLISHING A TRUST. Trusts are a powerful tool
in estate planning. They create legal and financial protection for
your assets, including real estate, investments, collections, proceeds
from life insurance, and other property of value. Creating a trust can
ensure your assets are managed and distributed as you want them to
be, both during your lifetime and after your death.

Unlike wills, trusts do not go through probate—the legal process that
transfers assets and pays debts to creditors after a death. Depending

on the financial details of your estate, bypassing probate can be of significant advantage, in money and time, to your beneficiaries. Trusts can also provide a way to:

- Reduce or eliminate gift and estate taxes

- Protect assets in your estate from some creditors

- Establish conditions and circumstances under which beneficiaries are allowed to use a portion, or all, of their bequest (such as reaching a certain age in adulthood)

- Direct how assets will be used to support minor and adult children

- Provide financial support for children and adults with special needs, without interfering with their access to federal and state financial assistance programs

- Give the trustee(s) you select the responsibility for managing your assets if you are unable to make financial decisions yourself

When you create a trust, you select a *trustee* to manage the trust's assets as you've directed. A trustee steps into your shoes and acts as your proxy. Make sure that you choose someone you trust with your money and important decisions, a person who will respect and carry out your intentions in your absence. The people you designate as trustees are those you feel fully confident understand your wishes and intentions and will act on your behalf as you would act yourself if you were able to.

You choose the beneficiaries of your trust, as well as the terms and conditions under which they will benefit from the trust assets. In addition to naming individuals, you can designate charities and other organizations as beneficiaries of a trust.

There are several different types of trusts, and selecting the right one for your estate will depend on your goals, budget, and financial circumstances. Trusts are a topic to discuss in depth with an estate planning attorney and your financial advisor.

⭐ *Gabrielle's Pro Tip*   Your life will continue to change and evolve as you move beyond your divorce and into your independent future. Revisit your estate plan every five years, or sooner if you anticipate or experience a major life change, including remarriage.

Remarriage, Cohabitation, and Blending Families After Divorce

Your life after divorce will be full of new experiences, new directions, new friends, and possibly a new love. It's exciting, fresh, and full of promise. As you're enjoying your new life, it's important to remain focused on protecting the financial autonomy and security you've worked hard to establish.

TAKE YOUR TIME. Be careful and mindful about getting into a committed relationship following divorce. Horror stories abound about post-divorce rebound relationships that happen too fast and are too good to be true. You've worked long and hard to achieve your independence and an open road into your future life. Give yourself some time to settle into that new life and acclimate to your hard-won freedom before you commit to another serious relationship.

> ✖ **DON'T** introduce your new romantic interest to your children until you know you're serious and committed.

KEEP YOUR FINANCES PRIVATE UNTIL YOU KNOW THE NEW INTEREST WELL. Make sure you are fully aware of your new partner's financial circumstances before you take their financial advice or give them access to your funds. You can enjoy each other's company while maintaining full financial independence and privacy about financial matters. A new partner who balks at this boundary, or who pushes you to share financial information quickly or before you feel completely ready, is not the right person for you and may be looking to take advantage.

✖ **DON'T** share too much about your financial situation until you know and trust your new partner well.

REMAIN FINANCIALLY INDEPENDENT. You've worked hard to achieve your financial freedom and independence. It's worth keeping in place, even (and especially) if you fall head over heels in love. Like your marriage, this new relationship or marriage may not last forever. Stay focused on supporting yourself and stay committed to your personal financial goals. Continue to manage your own finances and plan for your retirement, keep close tabs on your cash flow, and be realistic about your money.

✖ **DON'T** buy your new love expensive gifts or create unsustainable expectations.

UNDERSTAND HOW YOUR SUPPORT MAY CHANGE. Some states have laws that spousal support may terminate if you are cohabiting with a romantic partner for more than ninety days. Review your divorce agreement carefully for any indication that your support will change or terminate if you start living with a new partner. Be sure you know what changes are coming before you commit to cohabitating so you are not surprised.

🔥 *Red Flag* If divorce agreements are public documents in your state, a person can peruse your agreement to learn your financial information in order to target you. Even if your financial statement is impounded by the court, there is a lot of information in the body of the agreement that is available for someone who is looking for it. Be aware, be cautious, take your time getting to know new people in your life, and make sure you know your new romantic partner well before you provide them any access to your finances.

If you decide to remarry . . .

GET A PRENUPTIAL AGREEMENT IN PLACE. A prenuptial agreement allows you to establish the terms of your financial relationship with your new spouse, and how your assets and income will be treated if you eventually divorce. A prenuptial agreement can help you maintain your assets and income as separate property. By marrying again, you're entering into another business deal. A prenup is your opportunity to decide how that deal will end if you divorce down the road, rather than having your assets and income divided according to state divorce laws. A prenuptial agreement is a legal document, and to ensure it remains valid if one day it's challenged by your new spouse in court, work with your lawyer to confirm that it is drafted properly and covers all the circumstances and issues you need to address. Both you and your new spouse will need to agree to its terms in writing, and it is important that each of you has the agreement reviewed by your own attorneys.

CONSULT WITH AN ATTORNEY ABOUT ESTATE PLANNING FOR BLENDED FAMILIES. Thoughtful estate planning is essential for married couples who are blending families. It doesn't matter what you and your new spouse have discussed, if you don't have a written estate plan, state law will determine where everything goes when one of you dies.

In some states, for example, two-thirds of a decedent's estate will go to children from a prior marriage or relationship if there is no written estate plan. At the same time, a surviving spouse generally has the right to claim a share of a decedent's estate, typically one-third or one-half, if the decedent's written estate plan doesn't provide adequate support. To avoid any unintentional bequests or misunderstandings, you and your new spouse need an estate plan that clearly sets forth your intentions with respect to who gets your assets when you pass away.

🔥 *Red Flag* Naming your new spouse (or anyone else) as the beneficiary of your insurance policy, retirement accounts, or transfer-/pay-on-death accounts places that person in total control of these assets once you pass away. Your surviving spouse is free to leave those assets to their own children or even to a new spouse if they remarry. To protect your intentions, consider creating a trust to ensure that your assets transfer as you wish and are not changed after your death.

Estate planning in blended families can get very complex, and there's a lot of potential for conflict between surviving spouses and the deceased spouse's children. I had a client who was about to marry for the second time. Her family had owned an oceanfront property for generations. When not using it themselves, the family rented it out, which provided a great source of additional income. In the event she predeceased her new spouse, my client wanted them to have the rental income, but she didn't want them to be able to sell the family property. It was important to her that the home stay in the ownership of the family bloodline—her children. She wanted her new spouse to have an income from those assets and access to principal for medical expenses or other necessities, but she also wished to preserve as much of the principal as possible for her children. One option was to hold the property in trust, with her surviving spouse as an income beneficiary and her children designated to receive the asset at her spouse's death. This type of trust structure can seem like a simple solution. But it would have put her children in the uncomfortable position of having her new spouse (their stepparent) standing between them and their future inheritance. Ultimately, she decided to make her children beneficiaries of a life insurance policy that would be paid upon her death, which would give her kids the immediate inheritance and the liquidity they wanted, while the rest of the assets remained in trust for them until after her spouse died.

Key Takeaways and Next Steps

Your next steps? Go enjoy your life. Invest your time and attention in the relationships and experiences that bring you joy. Continue to use the financial tools and acumen you developed in your divorce—and ask for help, as often as you need, when you have financial and legal questions about your divorce agreement or any financial decisions. Live within your means and live to the fullest—you can do both at the same time, and you'll be richer for it in all ways.

ADDITIONAL RESOURCES

Financial Resources

To find qualified financial professionals, check credentials and complaint histories, and find information about financial planning and decision-making during and after a divorce:

Association of Divorce Financial Planners: *www.divorceandfinance.org*

Certified Financial Planner Board of Standards: *www.cfp.net*

Financial Industry Regulatory Authority: *www.brokercheck.com*

Institute for Divorce Financial Analysts: *www.institutedfa.org*

National Association of Certified Valuation Analysts: *www.nacva.com*

Women's Institute for Financial Education: *www.wife.org*

CREDIT REPORTING AGENCIES AND CREDIT REPORTS

TransUnion: *www.transunion.com*

Equifax: *www.equifax.com*

Experian: *www.experian.com*

www.annualcreditreport.com

APPS FOR TRACKING SHARED EXPENSES

CoParently: *www.coparently.com*

ExExpense: *www.exexpense.com*

Our Family Wizard: *www.ourfamilywizard.com*

SupportPay: *www.supportpay.com*

RESOURCES FOR ORGANIZING AND DOCUMENTING FINANCIAL INFORMATION

Dropbox: *www.dropbox.com*

Quicken: *www.quicken.com*

Legal Resources

For education about legal aspects of divorce, access to US states' divorce laws and resources, and access to US states' child support calculators:

Divorce Source: *www.divorcesource.com*

DivorceNet: *www.divorcenet.com*

All Law: *www.alllaw.com*

For help finding divorce and family law attorneys, mediators, and arbitrators; checking credentials and complaint histories; and educating yourself about legal issues related to divorce:

American Academy of Matrimonial Lawyers: *www.aaml.org*

American Arbitration Association: *www.adr.org*

Association of Attorney-Mediators: *www.attorney-mediators.org*

American Bar Association: *www.americanbar.org*

For information on mediators and arbitrators:

JAMS Mediation, Arbitration, and ADR Services: *www.jamsadr.com*